Lesley Herbert's Complete Book of

Sugar Flowers

A STYLISH DESIGN ON WHICH TO DISPLAY SOPHISTICATED
flowers. The stripes are applied by masking the
surface with tape, then airbrushing the colour.
Gold haberdashery trimming is attached with
softened flower paste to complete the simple, yet
effective, cake. See page 90 for flowers.

Lesley Herbert's Complete Book of

Sugar Flowers

MEREHURST

To my daughter Katie
and my son Marc, wishing you all the
happiness in the world.
With my love.

First published in 1995 by Merehurst Limited, Ferry House,
51–57 Lacy Road, Putney, London SW15 1PR

ISBN 1 85391 356 1

Edited by Bridget Jones
Designed by Maggie Aldred
Photography by Clive Streeter
Colour separation by Global Colour, Malaysia
Typeset by Litho Link Ltd, Welshpool, Powys
Printed in Italy by Milanostampa SpA

CONTENTS

NOTES ON USING THE RECIPES

For all recipes, quantities are given in metric, Imperial and cup measurements. Follow one set of measurements only as they are not interchangeable. Standard 5ml teaspoons and 15ml tablespoons are used. Australian readers, whose tablespoons measure 20ml, should adjust quantities accordingly. All spoon measures are assumed to be level unless otherwise stated. Eggs are a standard size 3 (medium).

An Introduction to Sugar Flowers

This chapter explains how to make and use flower paste, and it illustrates the equipment. Refer back to this information if in doubt about any basic methods. The flowers follow, arranged in alphabetical order. Each flower can be made without having to refer to methods on other pages — just follow the step-by-step photographs and read the instructions as you work. Finally, the third section brings the flowers together in classic arrangements and shows how to display them on cakes.

FLOWER PASTE

The best way to measure the fat and liquid glucose is to melt a small bowl of fat and the jar of liquid glucose in or over hot water, then take out the required amount with a clean measuring spoon.

*250g (8oz/1½ cups) bridal
icing (confectioners') sugar
1 sheet leaf gelatine
5ml (1 teaspoon) gum tragacanth
10ml (2 teaspoons) carboxymethyl cellulose
30g (1oz/6 teaspoons) egg white
5ml (1 teaspoon) liquid glucose (clear corn syrup),
warmed
5ml (1 teaspoon) white vegetable fat (shortening),
melted*

Set the oven at 150°C (300°F/Gas 2). Place the icing sugar in an ovenproof bowl, cover with foil and place in the oven for 15 minutes.

Soak the leaf gelatine in a bowl of cold water for 1-2 minutes, until softened. Lift the gelatine out of the bowl, draining away as much water as possible.

Warm the mixing bowl from an electric food mixer by filling it with hot water, emptying it and drying quickly. Place the hot sugar, gum tragacanth, carboxymethyl cellulose, egg white, gelatine and liquid glucose in the bowl. Mix on slow speed to blend the ingredients together, then increase the speed and mix until the flower paste is white and fluffy. Add the white vegetable fat and mix for a further 30 seconds.

Immediately after mixing the paste, place it in a polythene bag and store it in a small airtight container in the refrigerator until required. This paste can be used as soon as it is mixed but for best results it should be stored overnight.

USE

Cut a piece of paste from the block. Grease your hands with white vegetable fat (shortening) and knead the paste until it is pliable and stretchy. This flower paste is very strong, so it is recommended that you knead equal quantities of it and sugarpaste together. This will increase the amount of paste and extend the working time during which the paste will remain pliable when in use. Also, flowers made with the mixture of pastes will not dry to as brittle a finish as those made from flower paste alone, they are therefore less fragile, and easier to handle.

SOFTENED FLOWER PASTE

This is used as a glue when assembling petals and flowers. Place 30g (1oz) flower paste in a small screw-top jar and add 15ml (1 tablespoon) water. Place in the microwave – without the lid – or stand the jar in a saucepan of simmering water. Heat the mixture, stirring occasionally, until the paste

FLOWER TIP

If using regular icing (confectioners') sugar instead of bridal icing sugar, reduce the quantity to 230g (7½ oz / 1⅓ cup) as some icing sugar does not absorb as much liquid as others.

dissolves. If using the microwave, heat for 10 seconds at a time on full power or use defrost setting. Do not overheat the mixture or the sugars will crystallize and a skin will form. Remove from the heat. At first the mixture may still contain small lumps of paste; these will disperse or they may be pressed out using the back of a teaspoon. Leave the jar uncovered until the paste is cold. The glue is then ready for use. Adjust the consistency, if required, by adding more paste to thicken the glue or more water to thin it.

Mix the flower paste on slow speed at first, until the ingredients are blended together.

Making flower paste: accurate measuring and careful preparation are important for success.

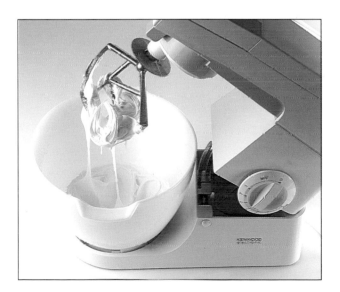

When the ingredients are combined, increase the speed and mix until the flower paste is white and fluffy.

The finished flower paste which has been wrapped and stored overnight in an airtight container.

To use the paste, cut off a piece and knead it until it is pliable. Wrap paste which is not being used to prevent it drying out.

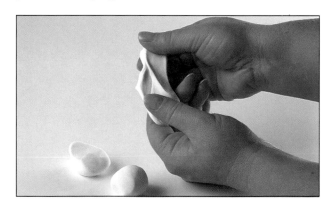

When it is first made, flower paste is too elastic but after standing and kneading it has a smooth, pliable and stretchy texture.

PROBLEM-SOLVING TIPS

Sticky Paste
- Add more white vegetable fat (shortening).
- Knead in more icing (confectioners') sugar.
- Too much liquid glucose (clear corn syrup) used.
- Quantities or method of recipe not followed correctly.

Paste Hard and Crumbly
- Insufficient kneading – knead the paste well.
- Dip the paste in egg white or water, then knead well.
- Add sugarpaste to the flower paste.
- Quantities or method of recipe not followed correctly.

Paste Short, not Stretchy
- Too much fat added.
- Carboxymethyl cellulose omitted or not enough added.
- Insufficient kneading – knead well.

Lumpy Paste
- Icing (confectioners') sugar crusted in packet.
- Paste left uncovered.
- Paste not stored in airtight container.

Jelly Spots
- Clear jelly spots in the paste indicate that the gelatine has not been mixed in properly.
- Knead small pieces of paste well to disperse the jelly spots.

Mouldy Paste
- Incorrect storage.
- Old paste, past its best.

Flower Paste not Setting
- Quantities of recipe not followed correctly.
- Too little gum tragacanth used.
- Too much sugarpaste added to flower paste.

GLAZING TECHNIQUES

STEAMING

Hold the dry flower or leaf in the steam of a boiling kettle until damp. The steam melts the powder food colouring enough to blend the colours together. After steaming, the paste dries to a silky shine. *Do not* steam flowers until they have thoroughly dried as the moisture will dissolve the paste.

SPRAY FAT OR GLAZE

Place the flowers or leaves on greaseproof paper (parchment) or absorbent kitchen paper and glaze with aerosol spray fat or edible glaze. Leave to dry. This gives a natural, long-lasting shine.

CONFECTIONERS' VARNISH

Leaves can be painted with this edible varnish or dipped into a pot of the varnish. The varnish gives a high-gloss finish which is perfect for berries and very glossy foliage. Brushes must be cleaned in an edible solvent after use.

POLLEN

Pollen is available in a variety of colours and its granular texture is also perfect for flower centres. Different coloured pollens can be mixed or powder food colouring can be added to produce a wide variety of tints and shades of colours.

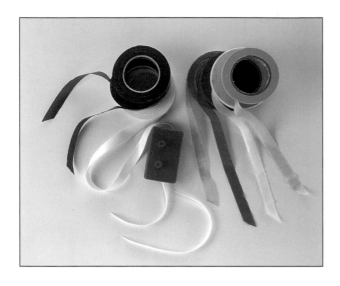

FLORISTRY TAPE AND CUTTER

There are two main types of floristry tape: paper tape, such as Stem Tex, or plastic tape, such as Parafilm. Both are available in many colours.

The cutter shown in the picture can be used to cut the tape into two or four equal widths.

When using floristry tape, cut the end at an angle and begin binding with the point of the tape – this will help to give the taping a neat start. It is important to stretch the tape to its maximum capacity to give a neat, delicate stem and it is only when well stretched that the tape sticks to itself and will not unwind.

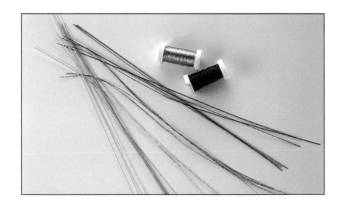

WIRES

The thickness of wire is expressed as a gauge number. The higher the gauge number, the softer and more pliable the wire; the lower the gauge number, the stiffer and less flexible the wire. Therefore use 33 gauge for small, light flowers and 24 gauge for large flowers.

There is a wide variety of wire available. Paper-covered wire is excellent for sugar flowers and it is available in 33, 32, 30, 28, 26 and 24 gauge as well as in a variety of colours.

Green plastic-coated floristry wire, which is available in different gauges and lengths, is usually used when assembling bouquets.

Silver or green reel wire is available in 32, 30 or 28 gauge; as for other wires, the thinnest most pliable wire is 32 gauge. This wire is used mainly for tiny flowers, such as jasmine, or for binding bouquets.

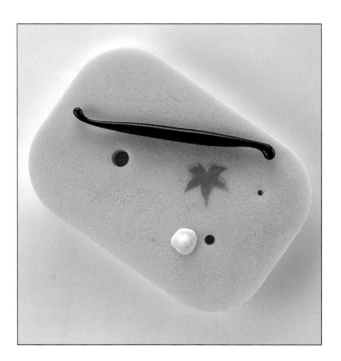

CEL PAD

This invaluable piece of equipment is used when shaping and smoothing petals. A cel pad has a non-stick surface on which the paste may be smoothed until paper thin without causing damaging. When making flowers with a cone-shaped back, the flowers can be inserted into the suitable hole so that the petals can be shaped without damaging the back of flower.

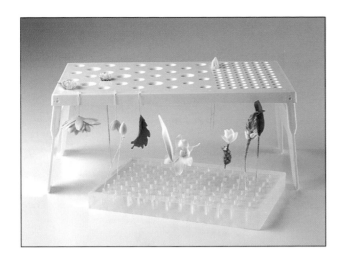

FLOWER STANDS

Both stands are useful for storing and carrying finished flowers. The versatile non-stick stand is washable and it will fold flat for easy storage when not in use. Flowers can be hung upside down from the stand or placed in the variety of formers to dry.

The perspex stand is used mainly to store completed flowers.

FOOD COLOURING

Any food colouring can be used to colour flower paste but concentrated liquid or paste will produce the best results, especially when dark or deep colours are required. Knead the colour through the paste with your fingertips.

POWDER FOOD COLOURING

Sometimes called petal dust or blossom tint, powder food colouring is brushed on dry flowers and foliage. The brush used is the key to success. A 1.5cm (¾ inch) flat Dalon brush is ideal. If the brush is too soft, the colour will not be even and the natural effect of shading will be difficult to achieve. If the brush is too stiff, the colour will flick across the paste without clinging where required.

Dip the brush into the powder food colouring, then tap it to remove excess. Brush petals from the edge to the centre of the flower or as described for individual effects with particular flowers.

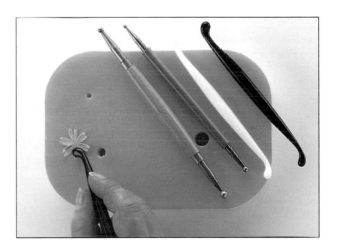

BONE AND BALL TOOLS

The bone or ball tool is used to smooth the edge of petals or to cup the centre and to smooth the edge outwards. Hold the tool half on the cel pad and half on the petal, then rub the paste gently.

To cup the petals make a circular movement with the tool on the centre of the petal.

VEINERS

There are two different-shaped veiners available. The black, *Jem*, veiner has a wide end and a narrow end. The wide end is used to flatten or frill a petal. The narrow end is used to mark a line on the petal.

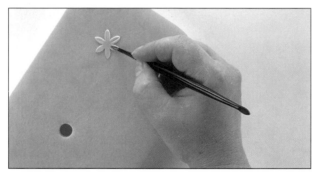

Place a piece of polythene over your index finger and hold the flower with your thumb, then press the tool against each petal in turn. The polythene will prevent the petal sticking to your finger. Alternatively, use the tool on the cel pad.

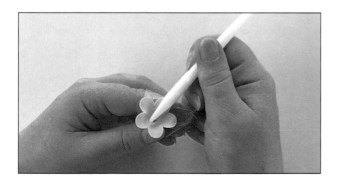

The white, *Orchard Products*, veiner has a pointed end, and a ball tool, with a removable line-textured cover. Use as for the black veining tool.

WOODEN DOWEL

Wooden dowel is available in different widths from do-it-yourself stores and cake decorators' suppliers. Cut the dowel to pencil-length pieces and use a pencil sharpener to form a point at one end. Grease the point of the dowel with white vegetable fat (shortening). The dowel is now ready to use when making hand-modelled flowers, such as azalea, or it may be used to roll out paste thinly.

NON-STICK BOARD AND ROLLING PIN

Available in a variety of sizes, a small smooth non-stick board and rolling pin are essential items of equipment for rolling out paste until it is extremely thin. Lightly grease the board with white vegetable fat (shortening). Roll out the paste until it is transparently thin.

THE FLOWERS

AGAPANTHUS

•

ANEMONE

•

ASTER

•

AZALEA

•

BLUE BELL

•

CARNATION

•

CHINCHERINCHEE

•

CHRYSANTHEMUM,
DOUBLE AND SINGLE

•

EUCALYPTUS

FORGET-ME-NOT

•

FREESIA

•

HOLLY

•

HONEYSUCKLE

•

IVY

•

JASMINE

•

LILY

•

LILY-OF-THE-VALLEY

•

MIMOSA

NARCISSUS

•

ORCHIDS, CYMBIDIUM
AND DENDROBIUM

•

PERUVIAN LILY

•

PINCUSHION FLOWER

•

POINSETTIA

•

PRIMROSE

•

ROSE

•

STEPHANOTIS

•

SWEET PEA

Summer roses in full bloom are a
popular choice for wedding cakes.
Half-open flowers and buds fill
out an arrangement.

13

AGAPANTHUS

AGAPANTHUS

Also known as African lily or blue African
lily, agapanthus is available in different shades
of blue and white.

Bud: Make a hook in a piece of white 33-gauge
wire. Roll a small ball of white paste. Thread the
straight end of the wire down through the paste
until the hook is just embedded in the ball. Roll the
tip of the paste between your index finger and
thumb to form a cone shape. Roll the bottom of the
cone to form a long thin stem at the base of the bud.
Rest the bud in the palm of your hand and mark
three lines on it using the pointed end of the veining
tool. Leave to dry.

Colouring Buds: Brush green powder food
colouring on the bottom of the bud and violet-
blue powder food colouring on the top of the bud.

Flower, opposite, top left: Using half-width white
parafilm tape, bind six fine stamens to a piece of
26-gauge white wire. Dip the stamens in violet-
blue powder food colouring. Bend the tip of the
wire over the binding to form a small hook.

Place a ball of white paste on your hand and roll

it with two fingers to form a cone. Grease the
point of a wooden dowel. Hold the rounded end
of the cone of paste between your finger and
thumb, and push the point of the dowel into the
paste by 1cm (½ inch). Pinch the paste gently on
the dowel to ensure it is evenly thick all around.

Using small sharp scissors, make six evenly spaced 5mm (¼ inch) long cuts to form petals. Pinch just the corners of each petal with your finger·and thumb, then squash each petal flat.

Cover your index finger with polythene, hold the flower in place with your thumb and gently flatten each petal against the polythene using the wide end of a veining tool. Place the flower on a cel pad. Place the point of a veining tool inside the flower, then mark each petal outwards with a line down the middle.

Paint softened paste on the hook of the prepared wire and thread it into the flower centre until the hook is firmly buried in the paste. Holding the flower upside down, roll the back of the paste between your finger and thumb until it forms a slim cone shape. Leave to dry.

Use liquid food colouring to paint a violet line down the centre of each petal. Brush violet-blue powder food colouring from the edge towards the centre of the flower. Using half-width green paper florists' tape, bind the wire of each bud and flower.

Bend the wires at a 90° angle 2.5-3.5 cm (1-1½ inch) from each flower and bud. Gently bend the flower or bud head up to form a natural curve. Bind the buds and flowers together at the point where the wire bends. Position the buds and flowers in a spiral effect with the stems. The flower and bud heads are not all at the same height.

ANEMONE

immediately dip it into black powder food colouring to give a velvet effect. Leave to dry.

Wind some violet-coloured cotton loosely around your index finger about fifteen times. Remove the cotton from your finger, in a hoop. Twist lengths of white or green 28-gauge wire through each end of the cotton hoop and pull them apart. Cut the cotton hoop in half to produce two bunches of stamens. Dip the tips of the cotton first in softened flower paste, then in black pollen. Leave to dry. Prepare three bunches of stamens and tape them around the centre of the anemone with half-width florists' tape.

Bend the top 1cm (½ inch) of a piece of 24-gauge wire at a 90° angle. Use pliers (tweezers) to twist the bent end of the wire around into a small hoop. Colour some paste black and roll a small piece into a ball. Push the hoop of wire into the ball and pinch the paste slightly to form a flat button shape which is firmly secured to the wire. Paint the anemone centre with softened flower paste and

FLOWER TIP
Bought stamens may be used instead of making your own. Attach them using tweezers while the paste is soft.

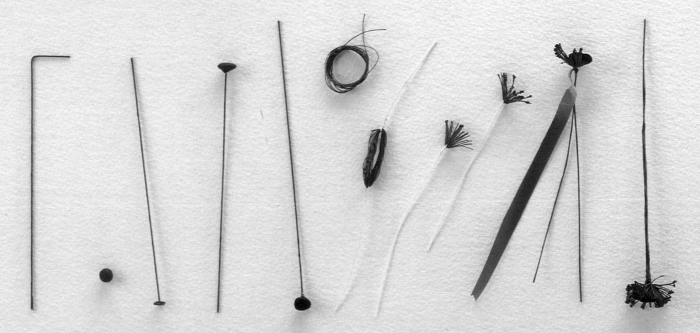

FLOWER TIP
The anemone does not have a calyx. A fern-like
leaf forms a little way down the stem. I have not
put these leaves on the sugar anemones as they
break very easily and are difficult to arrange.

Roll out violet paste as thinly as possible on a lightly greased board. Cut out the flower using a cutter or the template on page 138. Paint a little softened flower paste on the centre of the petals. Thread the wire from the stamens through the centre of the flower petals. Secure the petals while the flower is held upside down. Leave to dry with the petals supported.

Cut out a second flower shape, the same size or larger. Frill the edges of the paste and cup each petal. Paint softened paste on the centre and thread the wire through the flower centre. Rotate the wire so that petals lie over the gaps between the petals on the previous layer and secure the paste in place. Leave to dry.

Spray the flowers with an airbrush and liquid food colouring or dust the edges with powder food colouring, using a 1.5cm (¾ inch) brush.

ANEMONE
Also known as the wind flower.
Available in a variety of strong colours,
such as pink, red, purple, mauve and
mauve-blue as well as shades of white.

These flowers have large, delicate petals which become brittle when dry and they are very easily damaged. Therefore be especially careful when colouring or handling them.

Steam the flowers over a kettle and leave them to dry to give the paste a natural, translucent effect.

ASTER

Bend the top 1cm (½ inch) of a piece of 26-gauge wire at a 90° angle. Use pliers (tweezers) to twist the bent end of the wire around into a small hoop. Colour some flower paste pale yellow. Shape a small piece into a ball. Place the ball of paste on the palm of your hand and push the hooped end of the wire into it. Pinch the back of the paste over the wire to form a button shape for the flower centre. Brush softened paste on the top of the flower centre and dip it into yellow pollen. Leave to dry.

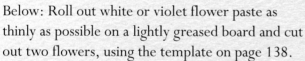

Below: Roll out white or violet flower paste as thinly as possible on a lightly greased board and cut out two flowers, using the template on page 138.

Place the flowers on a cel pad and use a scalpel to cut each petal into three pieces. Use a bone tool to gently stroke each petal from the point towards the centre to cup and thin the petals.

Brush softened paste on the centre of one petal and place the second petal on top. Cup the centre using a bone tool: this will shape the flower and stick the two layers together firmly. Paint softened paste on the back of the prepared flower centre, then thread the flower onto the wire, lifting the petals to give a natural effect.

The calyx is made by cutting three different sizes of daisy-shape flowers, see page 138, from thinly rolled green flower paste. Place the two largest sizes on a cel pad and cut the petals in half using a scalpel. Paint softened paste on the centres of the two largest pieces, then stick all three together. Place on a cel pad and cup the centre with a bone tool.

Paint softened flower paste on the calyx and thread it onto the back of the flower.

ASTER

Also known as Michaelmas daisies. There are many varieties of asters in a wide range of colours. Pinks, purple, mauve and white are common colours for blooms shown here.

Leaf: Roll a small sausage shape of cream flower paste and thread it onto a piece of green reel wire. Place the paste on a lightly greased board and gently roll it flat. Mark a central vein using the pointed end of a veining tool. Using the template on page 138, cut out the leaf, place on a cel pad and smooth the edges with a bone tool. Leave to dry. Brush with green powder food colouring. Spray with glaze.

Right: Bind the flower stems using half-width green parafilm tape, then bind the flowers together in groups of two or three with one leaf. Alternatively, use the flowers individually in arrangements.

AZALEA

AZALEA

Azaleas are part of the rhododendron
family. There are many varieties of these
plants with different leaves and flowers in a
dazzling array of colours.

Dip the ends of six pink stamens in brown
powder food colouring. Cut a piece of white 28-
gauge wire. Using half-width green parafilm tape,
bind the stamens to the wire making one stamen
longer than the others. Trim off the bottom of the
stamens to keep the flower stems thin before
binding with the remaining tape. Bend the tip of
the wire into a hook over the binding. Curl the
stamens by stroking with scissors.

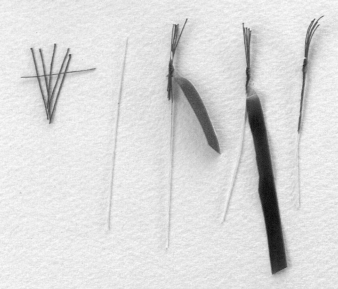

Colour flower paste deep rose pink. Make a small
ball of paste and place it on the palm of your hand.
Use two fingers to roll the paste into a cone shape.
Grease the point of a wooden dowel. Holding
the rounded end of the cone between your finger
and thumb, push the point of the dowel into the
paste by 1cm (½ inch). Pinch the paste gently on
the dowel to ensure it is evenly thick all around.
Using small, sharp scissors, make five evenly
spaced 5mm (¼ inch) long cuts into the cone.
Pinch together just the corners of each petal
between your finger and thumb. Squash each petal
flat. Place a piece of polythene over your index
finger. Hold the flower in place with your thumb
so that a petal rests on the polythene. Gently roll
the end of a white veining tool over the petal to
thin and texture the paste. Repeat for all petals.

Place the flower on a cel pad. Using the point of a white veining tool, mark a line down the centre of each petal – this will help to form a trumpet shape. Paint softened paste on the hook of the stamen wire and thread the straight end down into the flower centre until the hook is firmly buried in the paste. Holding the flower upside down, roll the back of the paste between your finger and thumb until the back forms a slim cone shape. Leave to dry. Brush the inside of the flower with rose-pink powder food colouring using a no. 5 paintbrush.

FLOWER TIP

These azaleas have groups of small leaves which are best made by the method shown instead of wiring many tiny leaves, a time-consuming task resulting in a thick, heavy stem of many wires.

Colour some paste leaf green. Roll out the paste as thinly as possible on a lightly greased board. Cut out the calyx, see template on page 138. Place the calyx on a cel pad and cup the centre with a ball or bone tool. Paint softened paste on the point at the back of the flower, thread the calyx on the wire and secure it to the flower. Use half-width brown paper florists' tape to bind two or three flowers together.

Leaves: Roll out green flower paste as thinly as possible on a lightly greased board. Cut out two groups of leaves, see page 138. Place one group on a cel pad; using a bone tool, cup each leaf from the point towards the centre. Then use the point of a veiner to mark a line down each leaf. Cut off several leaves from the second group – about half the group. Paint the cut edge with softened paste and position in the centre of a large group to give the impression that there are leaves of different sizes. Paint softened paste on the wire 1cm (½ inch) from the flowers, slide the leaves on and pinch the back of the paste to secure them.

BLUE BELL

BLUE BELL
These popular spring flowers are also available
in white and a mauve-pink shade.

Bud: Make a hook in a piece of 33-gauge wire.
Colour the paste with a mixture of leaf green and
violet food colouring. Make a small ball of paste.
Thread the wire down through the paste until the
hook is just under the surface. Roll the tip of the
paste between index finger and thumb to form a

cone shape. Leave to dry. Make three to seven
buds for each flower stem.

Dilute violet food colouring with water and
paint the bud using a no. 3 paintbrush. Paint two
thin lines down each bud. Leave to dry. Use half-
width green paper florists' tape to bind the wire
below the bud.

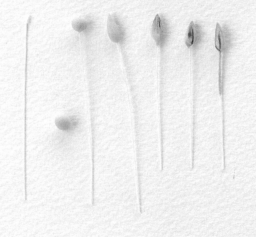

Flower: Paint the tip of a piece of 33-gauge wire
with violet food colouring. Colour the flower
paste lilac and roll a small ball of paste. Push the
centre of the ball of paste against the coloured
wire, 5mm (¼ inch) below the tip. Roll the paste
on the wire to form a small cone shape. Leave this
to dry.

Using half-width green paper florists' tape,
secure six fine yellow stamens to the wire just
below the paste. You may have to use tweezers to
position the fine stamens gently in a circle around
the wire.

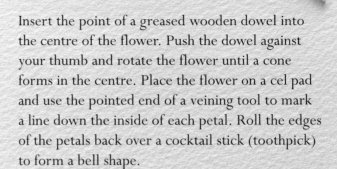

Roll a ball of lilac flower paste. Pinch the paste between thumb and finger, forming a stem and making a light-bulb shape. Keeping the stem in the middle, gently pinch and flatten the bulb of paste. This is known as a Mexican hat shape. Place on a lightly greased board and use a plastic dowel to roll out the paste as thinly as possible. Place the cutter, see page 138, over the stem and cut out the flower.

Insert the point of a greased wooden dowel into the centre of the flower. Push the dowel against your thumb and rotate the flower until a cone forms in the centre. Place the flower on a cel pad and use the pointed end of a veining tool to mark a line down the inside of each petal. Roll the edges of the petals back over a cocktail stick (toothpick) to form a bell shape.

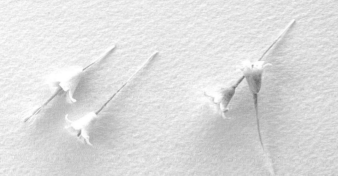

Thread the prepared stamens through the flower. Paint the green seed pod on the wire with softened paste and secure the flower to the wire. Hang upside down to dry.

Paint the petal tips and back of the flower with violet food colouring diluted with water. The colour dries to leave a delicate shine on the petals.

FLOWER TIP
A special rolling board can be purchased for rolling out the Mexican hat shape. Squash the ball of paste over one of the holes on the well-greased board, then roll it out. The hole forms the top of the hat shape.

Use half-width green paper florists' tape to bind several buds to a piece of white 24-gauge wire. Bind the flowers to the stem below the buds, so they can be gently bent. Notice that the flowers are staggered in position down the wire. Tape an extra piece of 24-gauge wire to the stem for strength and to make a longer stem.

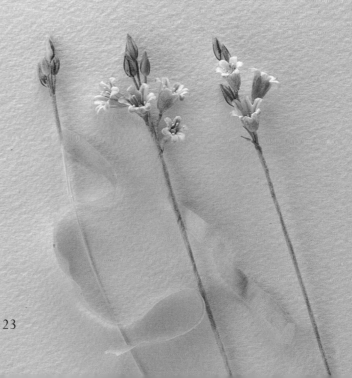

CARNATION

Calyx: Bend the top 1cm (½ inch) of a piece of 24-gauge wire at a 90° angle. Hold the angled wire with pliers (tweezers) and twist it to make a small spiral. Roll a ball of light green paste, then pinch it between thumb and finger, forming a stem and making a light-bulb shape. Keeping the stem in the middle, gently pinch and flatten the bulb of paste.

Place on a lightly greased board and use a plastic dowel to roll out the paste as thinly as possible. Place the cutter, see page 138, over the stem and cut out the calyx. Insert the point of a greased wooden dowel into the centre of the calyx. Push the dowel against your thumb and rotate the calyx until a cone forms in the centre. Place the calyx on a cel pad and use the wide end of a veining tool to mark a line down the inside of each petal. For texture, roll the outside of the calyx on a line veiner or a dried piece of corn-on-the-cob husk.

CARNATION

Popular bridal flowers, carnations are available in many colours and shades, including pink, red, yellow and white. The spray carnation shown has multiple flowers on the stem; single blooms may also be made by the same method.

Thread the prepared wire into the paste until the
spiral end sits inside the bottom of the calyx. Push
a small ball of paste inside the calyx, pressing
firmly with the end of a plastic dowel to hold the
wire securely in place. Dust the calyx from the top
down with green food colour. Leave until
thoroughly dry.

FLOWER TIP
Fresh carnations are full flowers with a
generous head of petals concealing the
stamens which do not show until the petals
wilt and droop.

Colour flower paste yellow. Roll out a piece of
paste as thinly as possible on a lightly greased
board. Cut out two petals, see page 138. Frill the
serrated edges of the petals by rolling a cocktail
stick (toothpick) back and forth over them. Paint
softened flower paste on one petal and place the
second petal on top.

Pinch the point of the petals to gather and pleat
the paste. Make five to seven petal pairs for each
flower. Cover the petals with polythene to prevent
them drying.

Brush inside the calyx with softened flower
paste. Place a petal inside the calyx and use the
wide end of a veining tool to squash it against the
inside of the calyx. Continue fixing petal pairs in
the calyx until the flower shape is formed. Paint
softened paste in the flower centre and push in
petals to give the full shape.

Roll out some light green paste and cut out a calyx shape, see page 138. Cut the separate sections and place on a cel pad, then smooth the edges. Brush two sections with softened paste and secure them to the base of the calyx. Bind the wire with half-width green florists' tape.

Bud: Make a hook at the end of 26-gauge wire. Roll a small ball of pale yellow paste. Thread the wire into the ball until the hook is just buried. Roll the tip of the paste to form a cone. Place on your hand and mark three or four lines using a veining tool. Leave to dry. Cut out calyx sections as above and stick to the bud base; dry. Brush with green colouring. Tape with half-width green florists' tape.

Leaf: Work a small ball of pale-yellow paste onto a piece of white 26-gauge wire in a sausage shape. Using a plastic dowel, roll out the paste on a lightly greased board working towards the tip of the leaf. Place the leaf on a cel pad and smooth the edge using a bone tool. Mark a vein down the centre using the pointed end of a veining tool. Allow to dry. Dust with blue-green powder food colouring. Tape the wire with half-width green paper florists' tape.

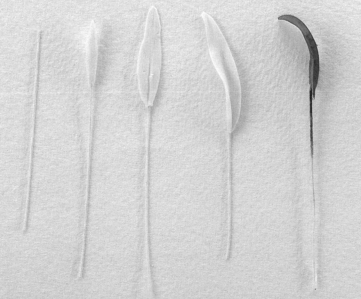

CHINCHERINCHEE

colouring. Take a tiny piece of the paste and roll it into a ball. Push the paste against the wire 3mm (⅛ inch) from the tip. Dip your thumb and index finger very lightly in cornflour (cornstarch) and roll the paste around the wire. Dip the tip of the wire in softened paste, then into pearl powder food colouring. Leave to dry. Using green half-width parafilm and keeping it stretched to a maximum, secure six stamens to the wire below the ball of paste. The heads of the stamens should be the same length as the centre wire.

Roll out white flower paste on a lightly greased board until transparently thin. Cut out two sets of petals, see page 138.

Cut a piece of white 28-gauge wire. Dip into softened paste by 1cm (½ inch). Colour some flower paste with moss-green paste food

Place both sets of petals on a cel pad, smooth the edges and cup the centres with a bone tool. Snip a 3mm (⅛ inch) cut between each petal. Paint softened paste in the centre of one set of petals, place the second set on top so the petals lie over

the gaps between the petals in the previous set. Gently dab the centre of the flower to cup it using a ball tool. Paint softened flower paste on the taped wire, just below the stamens. Thread the flower onto the wire.

Holding the flower upside down on the wire, gently pinch the back of the flower to secure it. The ball of green paste – the seed pod – in the centre of the flower helps anchor it on the wire. Pinch the top of each petal slightly to give the flower shape. Leave to dry. Make about six flowers for each completed stem. Repeat the flower stages, using the smaller template or cutter, see page 138.

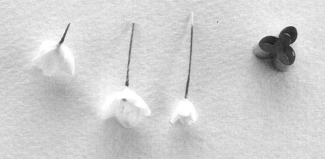

FLOWER TIP
The non-stick stand illustrated on page 11 is useful for supporting the flowers in the formers or hanging upside down around the edge while they are drying.

Buds: Bend a small hook in the end of a piece of white 28-gauge wire. Roll a small piece of white paste into a ball and slide it onto the wire until the hook is just buried in the paste. Roll the tip of the paste to a point to form a cone shape. The hook should not protrude. Pinch the bud on both sides to flatten its back. Leave to dry. Make about ten buds for each stem of chincerinchee. Brush the edges of the buds with apple-green powder food colouring.

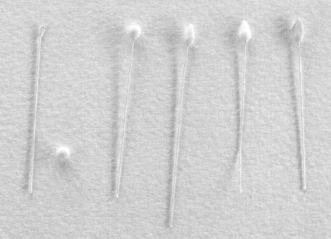

Flower Centres: Colour the paste very pale green. Make a ball and thread it onto a piece of 26-gauge wire with a small hook at the end until the hook is at the top of the paste. Place the paste in the palm of your hand and use three fingers of the other hand to roll the paste into a cone shape. Holding the cone upside down, use small pointed scissors to snip rows of small 'V' shapes, starting near the wire. Alternate the position of the cuts, so that they lie between and above gaps in preceding rows. Continue to the point of the cone. Bend the top of the paste gently. Leave to dry.

FLOWER TIP
A snowdrop-type flower may be made
following the method for chincherinchee. Use
a fresh snowdrop as a guide for details of
shape and form.

Brush the central buds or snips light green near
the bottom and darker green at the top. Using
half-width green paper florists' tape, bind four or
five buds to the flower stem. Stretching the tape as
much as possible, bind on a second row of buds,
alternating their positions in relation to the first
row. Snip off excess wires if the stem becomes
thick.

Bind the small flowers below the buds, leaving
their stems sufficiently long to give the finished
flower a cone shape. Bind the larger flowers to the
stem. Curve the wire on each flower to give a
natural shape. Bind all the wires together to form
the stem.

CHINCHERINCHEE
A spring flower with white blooms, this is also
known as Star of Bethlehem.

CHRYSANTHEMUM –
DOUBLE

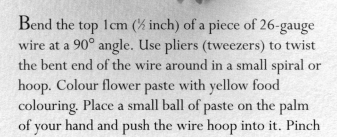

CHRYSANTHEMUM –
DOUBLE
There are many varieties of
blooms in delicate or strong shades of pink, red,
orange, yellow, gold and white. The blooms shown
here are a variety with full double flowers.

Bend the top 1cm (½ inch) of a piece of 26-gauge
wire at a 90° angle. Use pliers (tweezers) to twist
the bent end of the wire around in a small spiral or
hoop. Colour flower paste with yellow food
colouring. Place a small ball of paste on the palm
of your hand and push the wire hoop into it. Pinch

the back of the paste to secure it to the wire.
Leave to dry.

Roll out some yellow paste as thinly as possible
on a lightly greased board. Cut out two flowers
using the smallest, N6, cutter template, see page
139. Use a scalpel to cut each petal in half. Place
the flower on a cel pad and gently smooth each

petal with a bone or ball tool to thin the edges and
give the flower shape.

Brush softened paste over the paste on the
wire, then thread it through the flower and cup
the petals around the paste to form a tight bud.
Paint softened paste on the bud back and add the
second petal. Keep the flower tightly closed.

Colour some paste paprika. Knead equal portions of yellow and paprika flower paste together to give a pale orange paste. Roll out some pale orange paste and some yellow paste. Place the orange paste on top of the yellow paste and re-roll the double-layer paste as thinly as possible. Cut out one small, N6, flower and two larger, N5, flowers, see page 139. Cut the petals in half, smooth them with a bone tool and thread them onto the prepared buds, securing them with softened paste. The yellow paste must be placed underneath, on the back of the flower.

Repeat the process using paprika and yellow paste, cutting two larger, N4, flowers and one larger, N3, flower.

Cut out one N3 flower, place it on a cel pad and cup each petal – without cutting the paste – by smoothing from the tip towards the flower centre. Thread onto the wire, the flower should now appear to be opening. Make a further two N2

and two N1 flowers from paprika and yellow flower paste as before. Apply to the flower, securing with softened paste brushed on the back of the flower. Petals of graduated size are always applied – never add a petal which is smaller than the previous layer.

Calyx: Colour flower paste moss green and roll it out as thinly as possible on a lightly greased board. Cut out the three-part calyx using the three smallest flower cutters – N6, N5 and N4. Place on a cel pad and mark a line down each petal using the narrow end of a veining tool. Stick the three layers together using softened paste, then secure to the back of the flower. For the buds or part-open flowers you may have to use three of the smallest layers for the calyx.

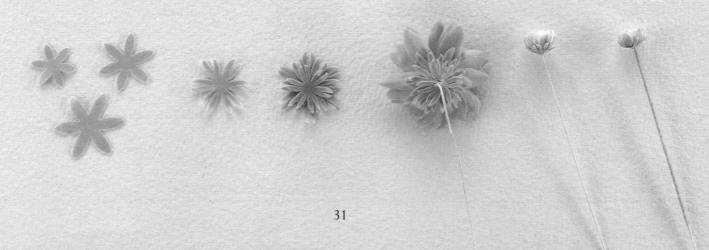

CHRYSANTHEMUM –
SINGLE

CHRYSANTHEMUM –
SINGLE
Although single chrysanthemums are available in a range of colours, the pastel blooms look most delicate.

Leaf: Colour a piece of flower paste green. Make a small ball of paste and roll it onto a piece of white 24-gauge wire. Pinch the paste flat and place it on a lightly greased board, then use a plastic dowel to roll it until the wire is just visible. Roll the paste above and on each side of the wire until thin, leaving the centre thicker. Use the cutter, see page 138, to cut out the leaf shape.

Press the leaf against a veiner to give it texture, then place it on a cel pad and smooth the edges using a bone tool. Leave to dry. Dust the front of the leaf with green powder food colouring. Place on a piece of greaseproof paper (parchment) and spray with glaze. Allow to dry.

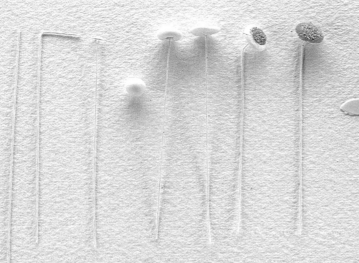

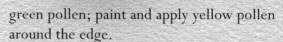

green pollen; paint and apply yellow pollen around the edge.

Cut out two flowers, see page 138, in pale pink paste. Place on a cel pad and mark a line down each petal. Smooth the edges with a bone tool. Paint softened paste on the centre of one flower, and position the second flower on top so that its petals lie above gaps below. Paint softened paste on the back of the centre, thread it on the wire and secure the flower firmly to the centre. Hang the flower upside down to dry.

Flower: Bend the top 1cm (½ inch) of a piece of 24-gauge wire at an angle of 90° and twist it into a small hoop. Roll a small ball of white paste and push the wire hoop into it. Pinch the paste into a flat button firmly secured to the wire; dry. Paint the button centre with softened paste and dip in

Paint softened paste on the back of the flower and thread the calyx onto the wire. Attach the calyx to the back of the flower.
Using half-width green paper florists' tape, bind a second piece of 26-gauge wire to the flower to strengthen the stem.

Using the three templates on page 138, cut out the calyx pieces from thinly rolled green paste. Place on a cel pad and use the wide end of a veining tool to mark a line down each petal. Turn the pieces over. Paint softened paste on the centre of the two largest pieces and place them on top of each other, alternating the position of the petals.

EUCALYPTUS

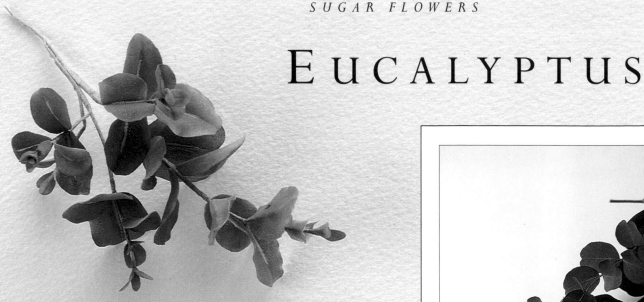

EUCALYPTUS
Also known as the gum tree. Eucalyptus is used in floristry for its attractive foliage, providing both shape and an interesting green colour.

Bud: Colour a piece of flower paste cream. The first three leaves are formed on one piece of 26-gauge wire. Push the wire into a ball of paste, then roll the paste between your index finger and thumb until secured to the wire. Flatten the paste on a lightly greased board using a plastic dowel. Make two tiny leaves without wires by forming cone-shaped pieces of paste and rolling them flat. Paint softened paste on the wire just below the paste and attach the pair of leaves to the wire. Leave to dry.

Leaf: Knead the cream paste well and form a ball. Cut a piece of 26-gauge wire. Push the wire into the ball of paste, nearly to the top. Roll the paste on the wire to form a sausage shape. Place the wired paste on a lightly greased board, and roll it flat until the wire is just visible.

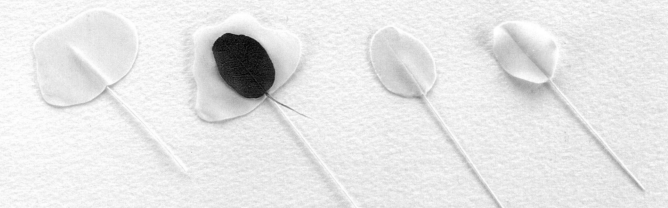

Using a plastic dowel, roll the paste on each side of and above the wire until it is very thin, leaving the centre thicker to keep the wire in place.

Using the template on page 139 or a fresh leaf as a guide, cut out the leaf using a scalpel. If you have used a template, mark a central vein down the leaf with the pointed end of a veining tool. A fresh leaf will impress its own vein on the paste. Place the leaf on a cel pad and use a bone tool to smooth the edge to give a slight shape but do not frill the edge.

Mix leaf-green and blue powder food colouring. Using a 1.5cm (¾ inch) flat paintbrush, colour the leaves all over, both front and back. Dampen the tip of a no. 5 paintbrush with water and brush the vein line, washing the brush occasionally to remove the colour leaving a pale natural-looking vein.

Make leaves of various sizes but remember always to make two of each size as the leaves grow naturally in pairs. Cut green paper florists' tape in half. Begin by binding the wire from the buds by 1cm (½ inch). Attach two slightly larger leaves, binding each leaf as close to the central stem as possible. Continue adding pairs of leaves until the required length of foliage is reached. As the leaves are taped to the stem, cut excess wire from the previous leaves as short as possible to prevent the main stem becoming too thick.

FLOWER TIP
The method shown here is suitable for making most foliage plants. It is worth experimenting with foliage as it is not put to full use in sugar arrangements.

FORGET-ME-NOT

FORGET-ME-NOT
Forget-me-nots are known for their bright
blue flowers. Some plants produce flowers of
mauve-blue and pink hues.

Buds: Colour some heather-pink and violet-blue
paste. Set aside a small piece of each colour, then
gradually add the remaining violet-blue paste to
the heather-pink paste. As you mix the pastes,
keep a piece of each shade before combining them
further. Take a very tiny piece of heather-pink

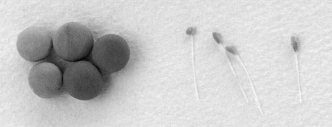

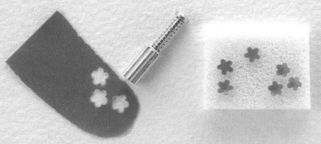

paste and roll it into a ball, then push the head of a
fine stamen against the centre. Roll the paste
between your finger and thumb until it covers the
stamen head and forms a cone shape with a
rounded top. Leave to dry. Using green royal icing
and a no. 0 piping tube (tip), pipe five small shells
from the stamen onto the paste to form the calyx.
Make five to nine buds using the three lightest-
coloured pastes for each spray of forget-me-nots.

Flower: Knead the violet-blue paste well and roll
it out as thinly as possible on a lightly greased
board – you should be able to read through the
paste if it is held over printed paper. Cut out the
flower using a small plunger cutter. To release the
flower, place the cutter on a piece of foam sponge

and push the spring-loaded plunger. Cut out
several flowers. Cup the flowers by rubbing their
centres in a circular movement using a small ball
tool.

FLOWER TIP
*It is important to cut out only a few flowers
and to shape them before the paste begins to
dry. Make the flowers using the three darkest-
coloured pastes.*

Use a large pin to make a hole in the centre of each flower and leave to dry. Using a no. 0 piping tube (tip), pipe a spot of yellow royal icing in the centre of each flower and thread a yellow stamen through so that the head sits in the icing. Pipe a small green circle around the stamen on the back of each flower for a calyx; dry.

Cut a length of green parafilm tape in half. Bind a bud to the end of a piece of 32-gauge wire. Bind a second bud just below the first; stretch the tape as much as possible. Continue binding the buds

to the wire, adding each just below the last.

When binding the flowers to the wire, leave a 5mm (¼ inch) length of stamen free between the flower head and stem. Continue adding flowers until the spray is as large as required. Brush blue powder food colouring on the edge of the flowers.

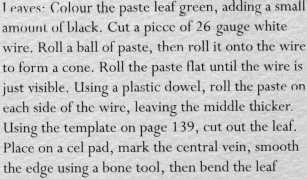

Leaves: Colour the paste leaf green, adding a small amount of black. Cut a piece of 26 gauge white wire. Roll a ball of paste, then roll it onto the wire to form a cone. Roll the paste flat until the wire is just visible. Using a plastic dowel, roll the paste on each side of the wire, leaving the middle thicker. Using the template on page 139, cut out the leaf. Place on a cel pad, mark the central vein, smooth the edge using a bone tool, then bend the leaf

gently and hang it upside down to dry. Brush brown powder food colouring on the tip of the leaf. Spray with fat to glaze.

Use half-width parafilm tape to bind the sprays of flowers to the leaves. The flower stems grow from the point where the leaves are attached to the stem. Tape the leaves and flowers onto a piece of 24-gauge wire to form a neat cluster of flowers and foliage.

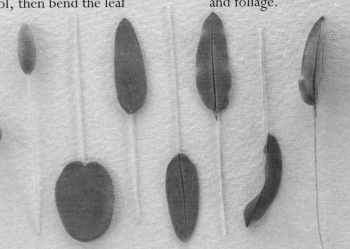

FREESIA

FREESIA
A spring flower, blooming in a range of
pinks, mauves, lilac, orange and yellow
colours that can be quite vibrant.

Cut the heads off a cream stamen, twist one
end and open out the paper from which the
stamen is made. Using small sharp scissors, cut
the paper into tiny strips. Work a small piece of
cream paste onto the end of a stamen in a boat
shape and mark a line down the centre using
the point of a veining tool. Make three more,
then tape them to a piece of 26-gauge wire,
2.5cm (1 inch) below their tips. Purchased
stamens can be used instead for speed.

Roll out the cream flower paste as thinly as
possible on a lightly greased board and cut out the
petals, see page 139. Place on a cel pad and use
the pointed end of a veining tool to mark three
lines on each petal. Smooth the edges and cup
each petal using a bone tool. Place under
polythene to prevent the paste drying.

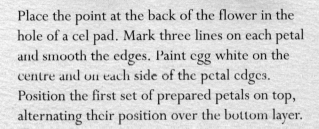

Roll a ball of well-kneaded cream paste. Pinch the paste between thumb and finger, forming a stem and making a light-bulb shape. Keeping the stem in the middle, gently pinch and flatten the bulb of paste. Place on a lightly greased board. Roll the paste as thinly as possible around the stem. Carefully lift the paste and turn it over – this is the back of the flower. Place the cutter over the paste and cut out the petals, pushing firmly for clean-cut edges.

Place the point at the back of the flower in the hole of a cel pad. Mark three lines on each petal and smooth the edges. Paint egg white on the centre and on each side of the petal edges. Position the first set of prepared petals on top, alternating their position over the bottom layer.

Make a small hole in the centre using a dowel, then carefully bring the inner three petals against the dowel. Secure the outer petals so that they almost cover the inner petals. Gently pinch the back of the flower over the dowel to shape the long slender back.

FLOWER TIP
Crocus flowers are similar to freesia and can be made by the same method. Use a fresh flower for reference.

Push the wired stamens through the flower until they are level with the petals. Work the back of the paste between your fingers until they form a fine stem, then remove any excess paste. Leave to dry. Dust yellow powder food colouring on the inside throat and the back of the stem.

Roll out some green paste and cut out two leaves using the tip of the freesia cutter. Place on a cel pad and smooth the edges with a bone tool. Mark a line down the centre with the point of a veining tool and brush egg white on the bottom edge.

Gradually add larger buds, trimming off the excess wire. Position the buds and flowers to the right and left of the stem. Using tweezers, gently shape the wire stem.

Colour the flowers if required – pink, lilac and yellow are popular. Dip the tip of a 1.5cm (¾ inch) brush into powder food colouring and tap it gently on a piece of absorbent kitchen paper to remove excess powder. Then dust the petals, brushing from the tip of the flower towards the stem. Colour the inside of the flower, again brushing from the edge inwards. Pass the finished flowers through the steam of a boiling kettle to enhance the colours and give a translucent effect.

Fold the leaf in half over the stem of the flower and trim off the excess paste from the side with scissors. Place a second leaf on the other side, then pinch the tips of the paste to form a calyx.

Buds: Make a small hook in 28-gauge wire. Thread the straight end of the wire down through a small ball of light green paste until the hook is just buried. Shape the top of the paste into a cone and work the bottom to form a long, slim back. Place in your hand, then mark three lines. Attach a calyx as for the flower.

Make five to seven buds for each flower, graduating the size and making the smaller ones a deeper green while the larger buds are cream. Cut green parafilm tape in half and trim the end to a point. Begin taping the smallest bud wires together.

FUCHSIA

FUCHSIA
Summer and autumn flowers with blooms
in shades of pink, red and purple, some with
very pale pink or white outer petals and
deeply coloured centres.

FLOWER TIP
*When cupping petals, place the paste on a cel
pad, use a bone tool and work in a circular
motion. If done on your hand, take care that
the paste does not stick.*

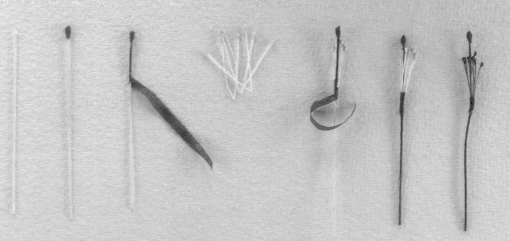

Flower: Colour the flower paste with red and
rose-pink paste food colouring. Cut a piece of 26-
gauge wire and roll a tiny ball of paste onto its tip
to form a cone shape. Tape the wire with a thin
strip of red paper florists' tape: this forms the
stigma. Select eight flat stamens and tape them to
the stigma. Dip the prepared stamens in red
powder food colouring.

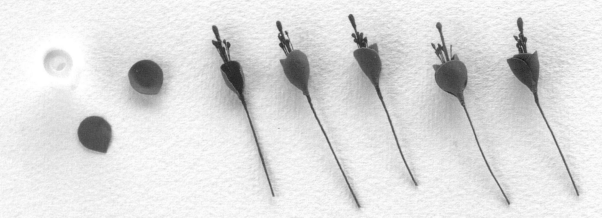

Roll out some deep pink flower paste as thinly as possible on a lightly greased board. Cut out four petals using the template, see page 139. Place the petals on a cel pad. Use a bone tool to smooth the edges and to cup the petals. Paint softened flower paste on the point of each petal and secure to the stamen wire. The stamens should stand proud of the petals. Position the second petal opposite the first petal. The centre of the third petal is positioned where the first two petals overlap. The fourth petal is secured opposite the third petal. These four inner petals are positioned to form a square with two pairs of opposite sides. Hang upside down to dry. Dust the fuschia petals from the petal edge down towards the wire with violet powder food colouring.

Pinch a ball of pink paste to make a stem and form a light-bulb shape. Pinch the bulb flat, keeping the stem in the middle. Place on a lightly greased board and roll as thinly as possible using a plastic dowel. Place the cutter over the stem and cut out the flower. Insert the point of a greased wooden dowel into the flower centre. Pushing the dowel against your thumb, rotate the flower until the centre forms a cone. Place on a cel pad and smooth the edges with a bone tool. Rub from point to centre to curl the petals.

Paint softened paste inside the flower and thread it on the wire. Thread a tiny ball of green paste on the wire below the flower to form a seed pod.

Bud: Make a hook in 33-gauge wire and thread the straight end through a ball of bright pink paste until the hook is just buried. Roll the tip of the paste into a cone. Roll the bottom of the paste to form the bud base. Place in your hand and mark lines down it. Thread on a tiny ball of green paste for a seed pod.

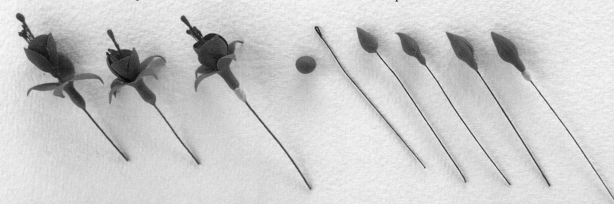

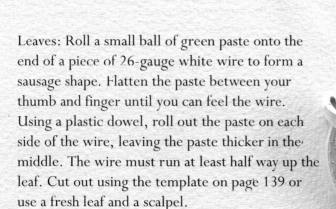

Leaves: Roll a small ball of green paste onto the end of a piece of 26-gauge white wire to form a sausage shape. Flatten the paste between your thumb and finger until you can feel the wire. Using a plastic dowel, roll out the paste on each side of the wire, leaving the paste thicker in the middle. The wire must run at least half way up the leaf. Cut out using the template on page 139 or use a fresh leaf and a scalpel.

This veining mould will texture the front and back of the leaf giving a very realistic effect. Place the leaf on the mould, fold the top of the mould over the leaf and apply gentle pressure. Place the leaf on a cel pad and smooth the edges with a bone tool. Leave to dry. Use red liquid food colouring to paint the central vein. Brush green powder food colouring on the leaf and pink on the edges. Steam the leaves to give them a natural shine.

Use half-width red florists' tape to bind the first 2.5cm (1 inch) of the stem of each leaf, bud and flower. Bind them together, with the flowers and buds forming from the point where a leaf is attached to the stem. Bend the stems into natural-looking curves – notice that the flowers bend over more as the buds open.

FLOWER TIP

The shape for the fuchsia cutters is shown with the templates on page 139. As the paste is rolled into a Mexican hat shape, with a point in the middle, you have to use a cutter, rather than a template, to cut out the flowers.

HOLLY

HOLLY

Winter foliage, especially useful for
Christmas arrangements. There are
variegiated types and an unusual yellow-
berried variety.

Leaf: Colour the flower paste with moss-green
paste food colouring. Roll out a large piece of
well-kneaded paste as thinly as possible on a
lightly greased board, then turn it over. Paint
short lines of softened paste on the bottom edge,
about 1.5cm (¾ inch) apart. Place a piece of 26-
gauge wire on each painted line. The length of the
wire laid on the paste will depend on the size of
the leaf: about 1cm (½ inch) makes a medium leaf.

FLOWER TIP
*Bind the leaves, staggering them down the
stem of holly. Berries form from a leaf joint,
so bind a bunch of berries and a leaf to the
main holly stem together.*

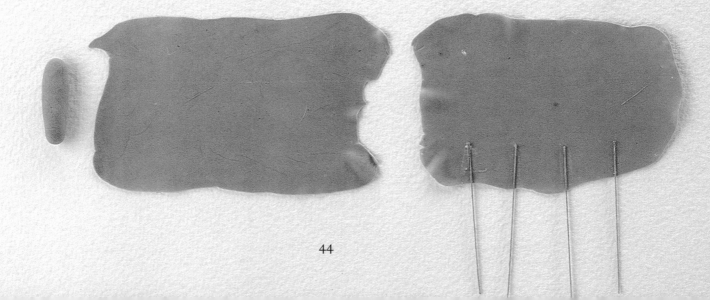

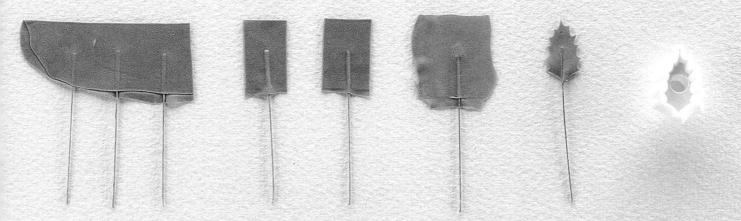

Fold the top of the paste over to sandwich the wires and apply gentle pressure with the palm of your hand to ensure the wires are secured between the paste. Cut the strip of paste between the wires to make equal sections and cover with polythene to prevent them drying. Place one piece of wired paste at a time on a lightly greased board and use a plastic dowel to roll each side and above the wire, leaving the paste thicker in the middle. Using a holly cutter, see page 139, cut out the leaf.

Push the leaf against a veiner to give texture, then place it on a cel pad and use a bone tool to rub the edges of the leaf. Pinch the back of the leaf and shape it naturally. Hang upside down to dry. Repeat with the other pieces of wired paste. Brush the front of the leaves with dark green powder food colouring. Dip the holly leaves into confectioners' glaze. Leave to dry.

Berries: Dip the heads of some stamens in black powder food colouring. Knead red paste food colouring into some flower paste and roll a small ball. Thread the stamen through the ball of paste, pulling gently until the tip is still visible. Roll the paste between your finger and thumb to shape it into an oval. Leave to dry. Dip the berry into confectioners' glaze and place on polythene to dry. Using half-width green parafilm tape, bind bunches of berries onto 26-gauge wire. Bind the first 2.5cm (1 inch) of wire from the leaves. Bind the leaves and berries, see tip, left.

HONEYSUCKLE

Flower: Bind five fine yellow stamens and one larger cream stamen to a piece of 28-gauge white wire using half-width white parafilm tape. Trim off excess stamen thread and bend the tip of the wire over the binding tape into a hook. Roll a small ball of pale cream flower paste, place on your hand and roll into a long cone using a finger. Grease the point of a wooden dowel and push the

HONEYSUCKLE
Wild or cultivated flowers in yellow, red, pink or orange, usually with two colours combined, for summer and autumn arrangements.

rounded end of the paste onto it. Pinch the paste onto the dowel to ensure it is evenly thick all around. Remove from the dowel.

Using small, sharp pointed scissors make two 1cm (½ inch) long cuts to form the back petal.

Make three small cuts in the remaining paste. Open out the four small and one large petals. Pinch the corners of each petal gently together to give a rounded effect. Hold all four small petals together and squash them flat between your finger and thumb. Squash the long petal flat. Place the flower on a cel pad and smooth the petal edges using a bone tool. Replace the flower on the dowel and pinch the back to form the trumpet.

Thread the stamen wire through the flower until the binding is embedded in the flower centre. Hold the flower upside down and use both index fingers to roll the paste onto the back of the wire. The back of the honeysuckle is long and narrow. Leave to dry. Brush inside the flower with yellow powder and the outside peach and pink.

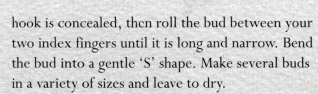

Buds: Roll a small ball of cream flower paste. Make a hook in a piece of 28-gauge white wire. Shape the ball of paste into a cone by placing it on the palm of your hand and rolling it with one finger. Thread the straight end of the wire into the cone until the hook is just below the surface of the paste. Pinch the top of the paste to ensure the hook is concealed, then roll the bud between your two index fingers until it is long and narrow. Bend the bud into a gentle 'S' shape. Make several buds in a variety of sizes and leave to dry.

Brush the buds with yellow powder food colouring, highlight them with a little peach and pink colour. Using half-width green paper florists' tape begin binding the buds together.

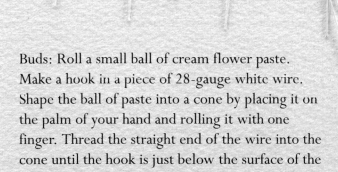

Left: Continue adding buds and flowers, binding them in the same place on the stem each time. It will be necessary to trim wires from the buds and flowers to keep the main stem delicate.

Leaves: Make a ball of green flower paste. Use your small finger to roll the middle of the ball to form a bone shape. Pinch each side of the bone shape flat and place on a lightly greased board. Roll each end of the paste to form two leaf shapes. The centre of the paste must remain thicker than the leaves. Place the leaves on a cel pad, smooth the edges with a bone tool and texture the leaves by pressing them onto a veiner or fresh leaf. Brush softened paste on the binding point of the spray of honeysuckle and thread the pair of leaves onto the wire. Gently pinch the back of the leaves to secure them firmly in place. Leave to dry.

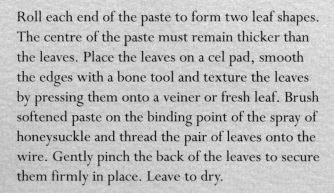

IVY

IVY

A creeping plant with shaped leaves which
may be variegated or a deep,
glossy green. The leaves also grow close
together, so can be bound in
pairs to cover some of the stems
in an arrangement.

Colour a piece of flower paste cream and roll
some into a ball. Roll the ball of paste onto a piece
of white 26-gauge wire, ensuring that it is firmly
attached. Pinch the paste flat, then place it on a
lightly greased board. Using a plastic dowel, roll
the paste on each side of the wire until thin, leave
the centre thicker to prevent the wire showing.
Sandwich the wired paste in a veiner and apply
gentle pressure. This type of veiner will texture

both sides of the leaf. Fresh ivy leaves do not have
prominent veins, therefore they do not make good
veiners. Use an ivy cutter, see page 139, or use a

scalpel to cut around the leaf shape made with the
veiner. Place the leaf on a cel pad and smooth the
edges using a bone tool.

Shape the leaf. Leave to dry. Mix leaf-green and blue powder food colouring together. Use a no. 5 paintbrush to brush the colour on the middle of the leaf. Always brush from the stem out towards the leaf points. Dab moss-green powder food colouring on the leaf to give a stippled effect. Place the leaves on a piece of greaseproof paper (parchment) and spray with fat or glaze. Leave to dry. Using half-width green paper florists' tape, bind 2.5cm (1 inch) from each leaf down the stem.

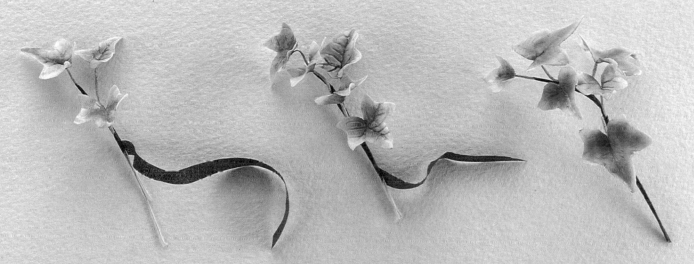

Use half-width brown florists' tape to bind the leaves onto the wire of the first leaf. As each leaf is added, trim off the wire from the last leaf as short as possible to prevent the stem becoming too thick. Occasionally, two leaves form at the same point on the stem. Place one leaf on top of the other and bend the wires together 1cm (½ inch) away from the leaves, then bind both to the stem at the same time. This gives a natural effect.

An alternative to brushing the leaves with natural colours is to paint them with gold food colouring. Allow to dry overnight before using. Wire gold leaves into stems as for green ones. Gold ivy leaves can look stunning, especially in Christmas arrangements.

JASMINE

JASMINE
Fragrant white summer jasmine is most popular; however, there are also winter varieties and pink or yellow-flowered types.

Make a very small ball of well-kneaded white paste. Roll the paste between your thumb and index finger to form a long, thin cone shape. Hollow the centre of the widest end of the cone using the greased point of a wooden dowel. Cut five evenly spaced 5mm (¼ inch) cuts around the paste to make petals. Pinch the tips of each petal together to shape them, then flatten the petals. Do not squash the hole in the middle as the deep throat is important for the correct shape. Place a

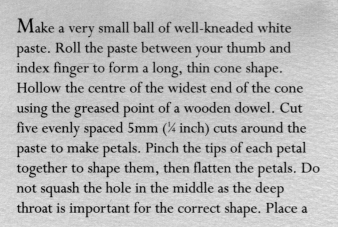

piece of polythene over your index finger and thin each petal in turn by resting it against the polythene and pushing the rounded end of a veining tool onto it several times. The plastic helps to prevent the flower from sticking.

Cut a length of plastic-covered reel wire and insert it through the flower centre from the base until it is just visible. Roll the back of the flower between both index fingers until it is as thin as possible. Remove excess paste.

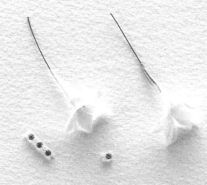

Sparkling sections of diamanté can be secured in the flower centre with a little softened paste to make the flowers sparkle. Dust the flowers with white lustre powder food colouring. Paint green food colouring on the stems.

Bud: Make a small ball of white paste. Cut some reel wire and make a tiny hook in the end. Thread the wire through the paste until the hook is just visible. Taper paste down the stem by working the paste between your index fingers until very thin. Shape the bud. Using small scissors, mark a cross in the bud to give the impression that petals are forming. Dust with white lustre powder food colouring and paint the calyx green.

Leaves: Push a ball of green flower paste onto white 28-gauge wire. Roll the paste into a sausage shape, ensuring it is firmly fixed to the wire. Flatten the paste on a lightly greased board using a plastic dowel, then roll out very thin on each side of and above the wire. Using the template, see page 139, cut out the leaf and mark the central vein. Place on a cel pad, smooth the edges using a bone tool and shape the leaf; dry.

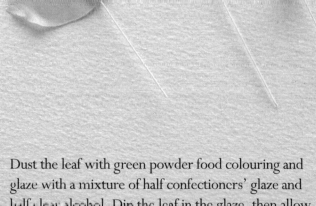

Dust the leaf with green powder food colouring and glaze with a mixture of half confectioners' glaze and half clear alcohol. Dip the leaf in the glaze, then allow to dry. Wire the leaves together with half-width green parafilm tape. Note that the largest leaf is on the top and smaller leaves are in pairs down the stem.

The flowers form from a leaf node. Small bunches of flowers or sprays of leaves are used in sugarcraft arrangements, alternatively individual flowers are used in bouquets.

LILY

LILY
Summer and autumn flowers, with trumpet-shaped blooms in a wide range of colours, from white with a hint of colour – such as yellow – to deep shades of pink, purple-pink and orange.

Bud: Cut a piece of white 24-gauge wire. Roll a piece of white paste into a sausage shape. Push the point of the wire into the paste nearly to the top. Place the bud on the palm of your hand and mark three lines from the top to the base using the pointed end of a veining tool. Leave to dry. Brush the bud with green powder food colouring.

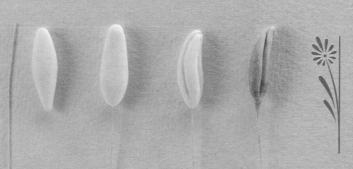

FLOWER TIP
When the lily first opens, the stamens are long with slim, bright yellow ends. As the flower matures the ends of the stamens change position and colour, becoming a bright paprika hue.

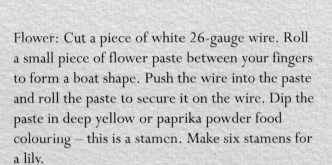

Flower: Cut a piece of white 26-gauge wire. Roll a small piece of flower paste between your fingers to form a boat shape. Push the wire into the paste and roll the paste to secure it on the wire. Dip the paste in deep yellow or paprika powder food colouring – this is a stamen. Make six stamens for a lily.

To make the stigma, work a ball of paste onto a piece of white 24-gauge wire. Roll the paste between your hands to form a long thin cone shape. Using tweezers, pinch the top of the paste into three equal sections. Brush the stigma with light green powder food colouring. Bind half-width green paper florists' tape several times around the base of the stigma to form a seed pod.

Bind the stamens to the wire just below the seed pod. The heads of the stamens should be positioned just below the tip of the stigma.

Work a large piece of white paste onto a piece of white 26-gauge wire in a long oval shape. Flatten the paste on a lightly greased board, then roll it out thinly until the wire is just visible. Using a plastic dowel, roll the paste on each side of and above the wire as thinly as possible, leaving the centre thicker. Using a template on page 140, cut out the petal with a scalpel. Sandwich the petal in a veiner to texture both sides of the paste.

Place the petal on a cel pad and smooth the edges with a bone tool, then shape it into a natural curve. Hang the petal upside down to dry. Cut out three inner and three outer petals using the templates on page 140; dry. Colour each petal before assembling the flower. Brush green powder food colouring from the centre base towards the tip of each petal, front and back. Brush pastel pink from the petal edge to the centre, front and back.

Bend the wire on the three inner petals at an angle of 120°. Use half-width green paper florists' tape to bind the petals to the stamens.

Bind the three outer petals so that they lie over the gaps between the inner petals. Bind all the wires together to form a strong stem.

Leaves: Work a large piece of white paste onto a piece of white 26-gauge wire to form a sausage shape. Roll the paste on a lightly greased board until the wire is just visible. Using a plastic dowel, roll the paste on each side of and above the wire as thinly as possible, leaving the centre thicker. Use the leaf template on page 140 and a scalpel to cut the paste. Place the leaf on a cel pad and use the pointed end of a veining tool to mark several lines along the paste. Smooth the edges with a bone tool, then shape the leaf with your fingertips. Leave to dry. Brush green powder food colouring on the front and back of the leaf.

PERUVIAN LILY
ALSTROEMERIA

Cut the heads off a cream stamen, twist one end and open out the paper from which the stamen is made. Using small sharp scissors, cut the paper into tiny strips – these form the stigma. Using half-width white parafilm tape, tape five yellow-headed stamens and the stigma to a piece of white 24-gauge wire. Trim off any excess lengths of stamen at the base of the taping. Curl the stamens over a blade of a pair of scissors. Dip the heads of the stamens in paprika powder food colouring.

Cut a piece of white 26-gauge wire. Push the wire into a large ball of white paste, nearly to the top. Roll the paste to form a long oval shape, then lay it on a lightly greased board and roll the paste flat until the wire is just visible. Using a plastic dowel, roll the paste on both sides of and above the wire until it is very thin. Leave the centre thicker to prevent the wire protruding. Using a fresh alstroemeria petal or the template on page 138, cut out the shape using a scalpel, ensuring that the wire runs down the middle. Place the petal on a cel pad and smooth the edges with a bone tool. Pinch the petal near the wire and shape the top gently, tilting it back; hang upside down to dry. Make three inner and three outer petals.

PERUVIAN LILY
Also known as alstroemeria. Available in a variety of colours, such as red, pink, orange, yellow and white with mottled or veined colouring features.

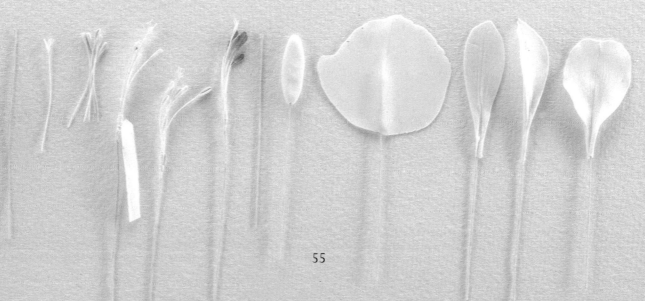

Brush yellow powder food colouring on the centre of each inner petal base and pastel-pink on the top of each petal. Use plum paste food colouring to paint small dashes radiating from the bottom of two of the inner petals. Brush a little green powder food colouring on the tip and centre back of all inner petals and yellow on the base of the three outer petals. Brush the top front and back of the outer petals with pastel-pink powder food colouring and green on the centre of each petal.

Using half-width green paper florists' tape, bind the two painted inner petals to the prepared stamens. Bend the wire of the third inner petal at an angle of about 120° and tape it to the flower to form a triangular shape. Bind the three outer petals to the alstroemeria, keeping the tape as close as possible to each petal so that the wire is concealed. The white and lemon flower shows one alternative method of colouring this bloom, which naturally blooms in a variety of colours.

Leaf: Make a small ball of white paste and cut a piece of white 26-gauge wire. Push the wire into the paste by 1cm (½ inch). Roll the ball of paste on the palm of your hand to form a sausage shape. Place the wired paste on a lightly greased board and roll it flat until the wire is just visible. Using a plastic dowel, roll the paste on each side of and above the wire until very thin. Leave the middle of the paste thicker.

Emboss the paste with a fresh leaf or veiner. Use a scalpel to cut out the leaf, using the template on page 138. Place the leaf on a cel pad and smooth the edges using a bone tool. Leave to dry. Brush the leaf with green petal dust. Place on a sheet of greaseproof paper (parchment) and spray with glaze. Leave to dry.

FLOWER TIP
To curl stamens over scissors, open the blades of the scissors and pull the blade along the stamens one at a time. The action must be firm so as to make the stamens curl but it must not be as hard as when curling ribbon, which is tougher than stamens.

Bud: Make a small ball of white paste. Bend a hook in a piece of white 26-gauge wire. Thread the straight end of the wire down through the paste until the hook is buried. Shape the top of the paste to form a cone. Roll the paste at the base of the cone between your index fingers to form the small seed pod.

Use the pointed end of a veining tool to mark three vertical lines at equal distance around the bud. Dust the bud with moss-green powder food colouring.

LILY-OF-THE-VALLEY

LILY-OF-THE-VALLEY
A delicate, white spring flower with
bold, glossy leaves.

Bud: Bend a hook at the end of a piece of green 26-gauge wire. Push the wire into a small ball of well-kneaded, pale green flower paste until the hook is embedded. Pinch the tip of the paste to cover the wire. Gently roll the paste into an oval shape between your finger and thumb. Make about five buds in a variety of sizes for each flower stem. Small buds are made in the deepest green paste, the larger ones are almost white; adjust the colour of the paste by kneading in more white paste as the smaller buds are completed.

Flower: Use half-width green parafilm tape to bind six stamens on a piece of green 26-gauge wire. Cut off excess stamen thread and keep the binding as thin as possible. Bend the tip of the wire over the binding to form a small hook; this will prevent the stamens and tape slipping off the wire when they are pulled through the flower.

Roll out some white paste on a lightly greased board – it should not be transparently thin; the thicker paste is necessary for shaping the flower. Cut out the flower, see page 140. Place the flower on a piece of foam sponge and cup each petal using a small ball tool. Turn the flower over then cup the centre by dabbing it with the ball tool.

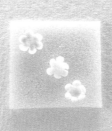

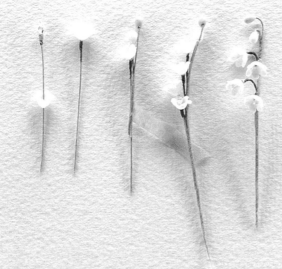

Paint softened flower paste on the binding of the wired stamen. Thread the flower onto the wire. Gently pinch the back of the flower onto the wire. Leave to dry. Use half-width green paper florists' tape to bind 1cm (½ inch) below each bud and flower. Begin with a small bud when binding the flowers together; as each bud or flower is added, cut out the previous wire to keep the main stem thin and delicate. When the required number of buds and flowers are wired, use tweezers to bend the wires so that the buds and flowers hang down.

Leaves: Roll a large piece of moss-green flower paste into a sausage shape and roll it flat on a lightly greased board. Use a plastic dowel to roll the sides and top of the paste as thinly as possible, leaving the centre thicker. Mark a central vein down the paste using the pointed end of a veining tool.

Using the template on page 140 cut out the leaf shape. Place the leaf on a cel pad. Smooth and thin

FLOWER TIP

Traditionally, lily of the-valley are arranged in silver favours or good-luck trinkets used to decorate wedding cakes.

the edge of the paste with a bone tool but do not frill it. Pinch the centre back of the leaf to give it a natural shape. Leave to dry. Brush with dark green powder food colouring and glaze with confectioners' varnish.

MIMOSA

Cut 3.5cm (1½ inch) lengths of green reel wire. Colour some flower paste yellow. For a realistic effect you will need deep-yellow and speckle pollen. Dip the end of a piece of wire into softened flower paste. Roll a small ball of paste

and push it onto the wire. Continue making small balls of paste in different sizes, from very tiny to about 5mm (¼ inch).

Paint the ball of paste with softened paste and dip it into the pollen. Dip the smallest-size balls in speckle pollen, the medium-size balls in a mixture of speckle and yellow, and the largest balls in deep-yellow pollen. Make about 24 balls for each spray. Leave to dry.

Cut green parafilm in half and use to bind the small speckled mimosa balls to the main stem wire.

MIMOSA
Also known as wattle or silver wattle, mimosa is a yellow, spring flower.

Tape on additional balls, keeping the tape stretched to its maximum so that it looks transparent. Trim the wire from each ball as additional balls are added to prevent the stem becoming thick.

Leaves, Left: Work a small ball of cream paste onto a piece of white 28-gauge wire in a sausage shape. The paste should stick firmly to the wire. If the paste does not stick well it could be too dry or not well-kneaded. Work quickly to prevent the paste from drying out. Flatten the paste.

Use a plastic dowel to roll out the paste on a lightly greased board, working from the wire to the tip of the leaf. Place the leaf on a cel pad and smooth the edge using a bone tool. Mark a vein down the centre using the pointed end of a veining

tool. Allow to dry. Dust the leaf with green powder food colouring and brush from the wire towards the point; brushing in this direction is less likely to cause damage. Spray the leaf with fat or glaze with varnish. Leave to dry.

Tape the bunches of mimosa balls and leaves together. Note that the mimosa balls grow from the point where a leaf joins the stem. Tape a leaf at the back of each bunch of mimosa, then tape both

to the main stem. Bend the wire so that the mimosa has a natural shape. If you need a long main stem, tape a firm 24-gauge wire into the base of leaf and mimosa ball stems for support.

NARCISSUS

Paint three stamens with softened flower paste and dip them in yellow pollen. Leave to dry. Tape the stamens to a piece of 26-gauge wire using green half-width florists' tape. Knead yellow, orange or cream flower paste well. Shape a small ball of paste into a cone. Use the greased point of a wooden dowel to hollow the centre of the cone. Place on a cel pad and thin using a veining tool. Put the flat end of the tool inside the cone and smooth it out to the edge; repeat all around the cone. To shape the trumpet, push the cone on a ball tool and open out the paste edge. Thread the stamens through the trumpet and roll the paste back to secure it to the wire. Remove excess paste; dry.

Below Left: Roll out paler yellow or cream paste as thinly as possible. Cut out the petals, see page 140. Mark lines on each using the pointed end of a veining tool. Smooth the edges with a bone tool. Paint softened paste on the centre of the petals and thread on the trumpet wire. Secure the petals; remove excess paste; dry.

Below Right: Take a ball of well-kneaded paste and shape it into a light-bulb shape between your thumb and index finger. Pinch out the bulb into a flat circle and roll it out finely on a lightly greased board using a plastic dowel.

Place the cutter over the paste and cut out the petals to form the back of the flower. Place the petals in the medium hole on a cel pad. Smooth the edges using a bone tool and mark several lines on each petal using the point of a veining tool.

NARCISSUS

Spring flowers, including the daffodil
and varieties of similar trumpet-centred blooms.
Yellow and white are the popular colours; there
are also peachy-pink types.

Make a hole in the centre of the petals using the greased point of a wooden dowel. Paint the centre with softened paste. Thread onto the flower wire, position the petals over gaps on the previous layer. Rub the flower back until long and slim — about

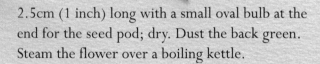

2.5cm (1 inch) long with a small oval bulb at the end for the seed pod; dry. Dust the back green. Steam the flower over a boiling kettle.

Buds: Left: Make a ball of yellow paste. Bend a small hook in the end of a piece of 26-gauge wire. Thread the straight end of the wire down through the paste until the hook is just buried. Shape the paste into a cone, moulding it down the wire. Remove the excess paste, leaving a small bulb to represent the seed pod. Mark three lines around the bud using a veining tool. Leave to dry. Colour the back of the bud with green powder food colouring and steam it over a boiling kettle.

Leaves: Colour some paste very pale green and roll a small ball. Roll the ball into a long thin sausage shape. Roll the paste on a lightly greased board, leaving the centre thicker than the edges. Using a fresh leaf or the template on page 140, cut

out the leaf with a scalpel. The fresh leaf will imprint its vein in the paste; if using a template, mark several lines with the point of a veining tool. Soften the edges with a bone tool but do not frill them. Leave to dry in a slightly curved position.

Dust the leaf with green powder colouring and steam it over a boiling kettle

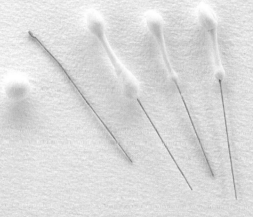

ORCHID
DENDROBIUM

ORCHID–
DENDROBIUM
This particular orchid is often available
white but it is also dyed, and available as a blue
flower. Make full use of the interesting-shaped
buds in arrangements.

The easiest way to model this orchid is to make a
mould from a fresh flower; alternatively, the
templates on page 141 can be used to cut out the
paste but templates will not contribute a natural
texture to the sugar flower.

Use a scalpel to carefully cut the petals off the
orchid. Make a mould of artists' or dental
modelling clay and embed the back of the orchid
column into it. Indent the centre of the mould to
give a natural curved shape. Roll out the clay to

5mm (¼ inch) deep, then embed the petals and
throat into the paste. The clay mould should now
be dried or baked following the manufacturer's
packet instructions.

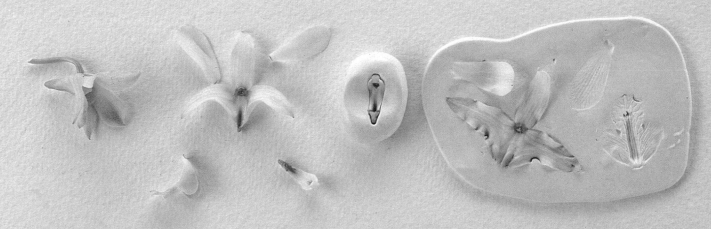

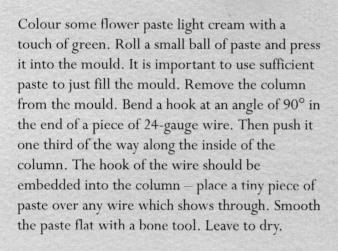

Colour some flower paste light cream with a touch of green. Roll a small ball of paste and press it into the mould. It is important to use sufficient paste to just fill the mould. Remove the column from the mould. Bend a hook at an angle of 90° in the end of a piece of 24-gauge wire. Then push it one third of the way along the inside of the column. The hook of the wire should be embedded into the column – place a tiny piece of paste over any wire which shows through. Smooth the paste flat with a bone tool. Leave to dry.

Roll out some flower paste on a lightly greased board to about 3mm (⅛ inch) thick. Roll each side and the top of the paste as thinly as possible, leaving the centre thicker. Push the paste against the throat section of the mould, with the thickest part of the paste in the centre. This will texture the orchid

throat. Cut out the paste using a scalpel and the templates on page 141, place it on a cel pad, then smooth the edges using a ball or bone tool to frill them slightly. Paint softened paste on the back of the prepared column and secure the throat with your fingertips; hang upside down to dry.

Roll out some paste as thinly as possible on a lightly greased board. Place the paste over the mould and gently rub it with your fingertips until an impression is formed. Cut out the petals using the templates and a scalpel, place them on a cel pad and smooth the edges using a bone tool. Paint softened paste on the centre of the back petals and position the side petals.

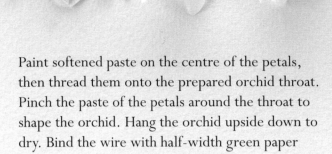

Paint softened paste on the centre of the petals, then thread them onto the prepared orchid throat. Pinch the paste of the petals around the throat to shape the orchid. Hang the orchid upside down to dry. Bind the wire with half-width green paper florists' tape.

FLOWER TIP
By using a fresh flower and modelling clay to make a mould, then baking it following the manufacturer's instructions, you will have a permanent mould in which to shape orchids. This same technique can be used for other fairly large flowers of the same type and you can build up a set of moulds for flowers which you are likely to make repeatedly.

Bud: Make a hook in a piece of white 24-gauge wire. Colour some flower paste light green or cream and roll a small ball. Thread the straight end of the wire down through the paste until the hook is just buried. Roll the tip of the paste between your thumb and index finger to form a cone shape, then roll one side of the cone near to the wire to form the bud shape. Pinch the points of the bud and bend it to form an 'S' shape. Make buds of different sizes and leave to dry.

Assembling Stems of Orchids: Use half-width green paper florists' tape to bind the wires of the buds. Bind the buds together, beginning with the smallest, gradually getting larger and staggering them down the stem. Carefully bend the wire of the orchid flower, then bind it to the stem. Orchid flowers are often used singly in bouquets, not wired onto a stem with the bud.

ORCHID
CYMBIDIUM

ORCHID –
CYMBIDIUM
An exotic flower available in a vast range of
colours and shades, including red, pink,
orange, yellow and purple.

Flower: Make a mould from artists' or dental
modelling clay. Carefully take a fresh orchid apart
and press the column from the flower centre into the
mould. Alternatively, use a bought orchid former.

Make a ball of well-kneaded cream flower
paste. Do not use too much paste which will
overfill the mould. Roll the paste into a bone
shape using your index finger, then push it into the
mould. Use a bone tool to hollow the paste
slightly, then remove it from the mould. Insert a
piece of 26-gauge wire into the flat end of the
paste. Leave to dry.

Brush the column on both sides with plum
powder food colouring. Brush green colour on the
back edge, towards the front of the column. Use
plum paste food colouring to paint dots on the
inside of the column.

Throat: Colour some flower paste cream and roll a small ball. Roll the paste flat on a lightly greased board. Leaving the centre thicker, then roll the edges and top of the paste as thinly as possible. Cut out the labellum with a scalpel, see page 140. Paint softened paste down the middle of the

labellum. Roll a thin cone shape of yellow paste, long enough to fit from the point to the end of the widest part of the labellum. Place the yellow paste in position. Lay the labellum on a cel pad and mark a line down the centre of the yellow paste, marking it into two without cutting through.

Left: Frill the lip of the labellum by smoothing it with a bone tool, then cup each side of the lip. Paint softened paste on the narrow part of the labellum and pinch both sides onto the wired column. Leave to dry. Use plum paste food colouring to paint large dots on the lip. Brush the edge of the lip with plum powder food colouring.

Petals, Below: Push a piece of white 26-gauge wire into a large ball of cream paste, until the wire is nearly at the top of the paste. Roll the paste into a sausage shape. Place the paste on a lightly greased board and roll it flat until the wire is just visible. Using a plastic dowel, roll the paste on each side of and above the wire until very thin.

Using a fresh orchid petal or the template on page 140, cut out the shape with a scalpel. Place the petal on a cel pad and smooth the edges with a bone tool. Shape the petals into a natural curve with your thumb and fingers. If possible, leave to dry over a fresh orchid petal to get a perfect shape; alternatively, hang the petals upside down to dry.

Make four more petals, using the appropriate
templates, see page 140. Take care to shape the
petals accurately to obtain a right and left side to
the flower. Leave to dry. Brush plum powder food
colouring from the wire down the centre of each
petal. Use plum paste food colouring to paint lines
of tiny dots on the front and back.

Use half-width green paper florists' tape to bind
the two side petals to the labellum. Bend the wire
of the two bottom petals at an angle of 90° as
close as possible to the paste; then bind them to
the orchid. Bind the top petal in position. Tape the
wires together to form a strong stem.

PINCUSHION FLOWER
SCABIOUS

PINCUSHION FLOWER
Also known as scabious, the
blooms can be made in white or pale yellow
as well as the bright blue shown here or a
more mauve-blue shade.

FLOWER TIP
*When using stamens, often only the heads are
required; collect the thread left for making
your own stamens and flower centres.*

Buds: Buds are made by binding five or six bunches of seed heads together without the cotton stamens. Make the seed heads following the instructions overleaf. Brush them with green powder food colouring. Make a calyx as for the flower and secure it to the back of the bunch of seed heads.

Roll a small ball of paste on the end of a stamen thread to form a small cone shape. Make about 36 of these seed heads for each flower centre. Leave to dry. Using half-width green paper florists' tape, bind about six seed heads to a piece of white 28-gauge wire. Bend the point of the wire over the tape to form a small hook and prevent the seed heads and tape slipping off the wire. Dust the seed heads with green and plum powder food colouring.

FLOWER TIP
It is far cheaper and quicker to make bunches of stamens than buying and using commercial stamens.

Twist some white cotton around two fingers about 15 times. Hook a piece of 28-gauge wire through the cotton loops and twist it firmly twice. Cut off the short ends of the wire. Hook some wire through the other end of the cotton loop and twist it as before. Cut the cotton in half to make two bunches of stamens.

Flower Centre: Use half-width green paper florists' tape to bind the stamens to the seed heads. Bind six bunches of seed heads and two bunches of cotton stamens together to make the centre of the scabious; use tweezers to carefully ease the cotton between the seed heads. Trim the cotton level slightly above the seed heads.

Above: Roll out some white paste as thinly as possible on a lightly greased board. Cut out the inside petals, see page 141. Place the petals on a cel pad and frill the edges by rubbing with the wide end of a veining tool. Paint softened paste on the

back of the flower centre, slide the petals onto the wire and secure in place. Leave to dry. Dust the petals with violet and blue powder food colouring. Cut out two larger flowers, see page 141.

Right: Place the larger flowers on a cel pad and frill the petals using the wide end of a veining tool. Paint softened paste on the centre of the first flower. Place the second flower on top alternating the petals above those of the first flower.

Below: Brush softened paste on the back of the flower, then slide the petals onto the wire and hang the flower upside down to dry. Dust the petals from the edge towards the centre with violet and blue powder food colourings.

Colour some flower paste dark green. Roll out the paste as thinly as possible on a lightly greased

board. Cut out the calyx, see page 141. Place the calyx on a cel pad, smooth the edges with a bone tool and mark a line down each petal using the pointed end of a veining tool. Paint softened paste on the back of the flower. Thread the calyx onto the wire and secure to the back of the flower.

POINSETTIA

FLOWER TIP

Stamens for poinsettia can be purchased but better, more realistic, results can be obtained by making them.

POINSETTIA

A winter plant with bright red bracts. Ideal for Christmas arrangements.

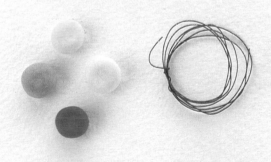

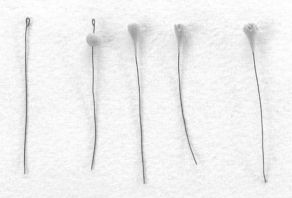

Colour three portions of flower paste: red, green and yellow. Mix a portion of white paste with some green and yellow to make a pale green. You need a larger portion of red and dark green paste. Cut nine 7.5cm (3 inch) pieces of green reel wire. Make a small hook in the end of each piece. Knead the dark green paste and make a small ball, then thread it onto a piece of wire until the hook is buried in it. Shape the paste into a cone and flatten the top slightly. Use small pointed scissors to snip small 'V' cuts around the outside edge of the cone. Continue snipping the paste around the cone and into the centre to make a bud. It is easier to hold the cone upside down to do this.

Make a tiny ball of yellow paste and roll it into a boat shape, then place on a cel pad. Push the flat end of a veining tool onto the yellow paste to shape it into a small leaf. Paint the tip on the bud with red food colouring and attach the small yellow leaf just below it, smoothing the paste onto the wire. Leave to dry. You will need about nine of these. Roll a ball of red paste into a sausage shape, then push a piece of white 26-gauge wire into it by 1cm (½ inch), making sure it is securely embedded. Place the wired paste on a lightly greased board and roll it flat until the wire is just visible.

Use a plastic dowel to roll the paste on each side of and above the wire until it is very thin. Leave the central paste thicker to ensure the leaf is secure on the wire. Trace around a fresh poinsettia bract to make a template to cut out the paste. Use a textured veiner to mark the bract, positioning the central vein just to one side of the wire. Apply gentle pressure on the veiner top with the palm of your hand, then remove the bract which will be veined both sides. Place on a cel pad and smooth the edges with a bone tool, using gentle pressure so as not to frill the paste. Shape the leaf and leave to dry.

The poinsettia does not have a set number of bracts; make two or three of each size of bract. The size of the poinsettia will depend on the cutters selected.

Small pale green leaves grow around the centre. Paint the veins with diluted red food colouring using a fine paintbrush; brush the edges with green powder food colouring. Dust all the red

bracts with red powder food colouring and brush green on their tips. Bind all the wires with half-width red paper florists' tape.

Bind three buds together. Bind three bunches of buds together with three leaves to form the centre of the poinsettia. Bend each red bract wire at an angle of 90° 1cm (½ inch) down the stem. Use half-width green paper florists' tape to bind the smallest bracts in place first. Continue taping down the wire, graduating the size of the bracts. Tape the leaves to the poinsettia in the same way.

FLOWER TIP
To make leaves for a poinsettia, use the same shape as for a bract and cut it out in green paste. Dust with a hint of red so that the leaves blend with the colour of the bracts.

PRIMROSE

Colour the paste melon yellow. Shape a well-kneaded piece into a ball. Roll it into a cone on the palm of your hand. Push a lightly greased dowel into the wide end of the cone and hollow the centre. Use small scissors to make five 5mm (¼ inch) cuts to give five petals. Snip each petal by 3mm (⅛ inch) down the centre to make five double petals. Pinch the corners of the petals sideways to round them, then open out the flower. Squash each double petal between your thumb and index finger. Place a piece of polythene over your index finger, support the flower with a petal on the polythene and push the flat end of a veining tool several times on the petal to thin and enlarge it. Repeat with all the petals.

FLOWER TIP
To make primulas in bright colours, use a lighter-coloured paste and dust to the required depth before putting on the calyx. This gives a more delicate result than using a dark paste.

Make a small hook in a piece of 26-gauge wire and thread it through the centre of the flower until the hook embeds itself in the paste but is slightly visible. Rub the back of the flower between both index fingers to shape and thin it. Remove excess paste. Use tweezers to insert one green or yellow stamen in the centre of the flower. Paint a triangle of yellow food colouring on each petal from the centre.

Calyx: Colour some paste pale green and roll a ball shape. Work the top of the paste between your finger and thumb to make a light bulb shape. Pinch the bulb of paste, keeping the point in the middle, until thin. Use a plastic dowel to roll out the paste as thinly as possible on a lightly greased board, working from the stem out to the edge. Cut out with a calyx cutter, keeping the stem in the middle. Make a hole in the centre using the point of a wooden dowel and gently pinch the back of the calyx over the dowel until the petals are straight and the inside of the calyx is hollow. Mark a line down each of the five parts of the calyx. Insert the flower wire through the calyx and secure the calyx at the back of the flower. Leave to dry.

Leaves: Work a ball of cream paste on a piece of 26-gauge wire. Gently flatten the paste, then roll it out on a lightly greased board until the wire is just visible. Use the template on page 141 and a scalpel to cut out the leaf. Grease a fresh leaf or rubber veiner, then push the paste against the veiner, taking care not to apply too much pressure near the wire. Place the leaf on a cel pad, frill the edge by gently smoothing it with a bone tool. Leave to dry. Use green powder food colouring and a 1.5cm (¾ inch) dusting brush to colour the front and back of the leaf, leaving the central vein cream. If some of the colour goes over the vein, dampen a no. 3 or 4 paintbrush and gently brush the colour away. Hold over the steam of a boiling kettle to set the colour and give a sheen; dry.

PRIMROSE

Yellow or paler cream and yellow are the colours for the primrose; however the same shape flowers can be made in a wide variety of colours, such as mauve, red, purple or violet.

STEPHANOTIS

STEPHANOTIS

A tropical plant grown in cooler climates
as a fragrant houseplant. An all-season
candidate for sugar-flower arrangements in
which the distinct white flowers show well
against the glossy leaves.

Leaf: Work a large piece of green paste onto a
piece of green 26-gauge wire. Roll the paste out
thinly on a lightly greased board until the wire is
just visible. Using a plastic dowel, roll each side of
the paste thin. Cut out the leaf, see page 141.
Place the leaf on a cel pad and mark veins using
the pointed end of a veining tool. Smooth the leaf
edge using a bone tool, shape it and hang upside
down to dry. Brush the front of the leaf with
green powder food colouring. Varnish the leaf by
painting with confectioners' glaze. Leave to dry,
then paint with a second coat of varnish.

Roll a ball of well-kneaded white flower paste, then roll the centre with your index finger to form a bone shape. Use the point of a greased dowel to hollow out the widest end of the paste.

Remove from the dowel, then use small sharp scissors to make five equally spaced 1cm (½ inch) cuts around the paste. Pinch just the corners of each petal between your thumb and index finger. Squash each petal flat between your thumb and finger to make the paste thinner. Place a piece of polythene over your index finger. Rest each petal in turn on the polythene, then roll a cocktail stick (toothpick) from the centre to the side of the petals to enlarge them and make the paste transparently thin. Rolling the cocktail stick from one side only across the petal will mis-shape the flower. Insert a cocktail stick into the centre of the flower and gently pinch the back of the flower.

Above: Make a small hook in green 26-gauge wire. Thread the wire through the flower until the hook is embedded. Fold the corners of each petal back to give shape. Hang upside down to dry. Use liquid food colouring to paint pale green lines on the back of the flower. Brush lemon powder in the throat of the flower.

Calyx: Roll out green paste as thin as possible. Cut out the calyx, see page 141. Place on a cel pad; cup the centre using a ball tool. Paint softened paste on the centre and thread it on the flower.

Bud: Make a ball of white paste and roll it into a bone shape. Make a hook at the end of a piece of 26-gauge wire, then push it into the paste until the hook is firmly embedded. Gently pinch the tip of the paste to form a bullet shape. Place the bud in the palm of your hand and mark five indents by stroking the paste towards the tip of the bud with the flat end of a veining tool. Leave to dry. Paint green lines on the long stem-part using liquid food colouring. Cut out a calyx, shape it with a ball tool and secure to the bud.

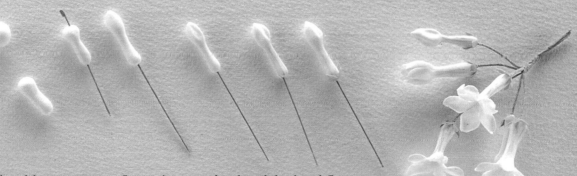

Sprays: Use half-width green paper florists' tape to bind each bud and flower stem.
Tape bunches of buds and flowers together – note that the flower forms from a leaf node.

SUMMER ROSES

Leaves: Cut lengths of white 26-gauge wire. Work a small ball of light green paste onto a piece of wire. Flatten the paste until you can feel the wire. Using a plastic dowel, roll the paste on each side of the wire, leaving the paste thicker over the wire. Use a cutter or cut around a fresh leaf. The wire must be at least half way up the leaf. Use a double veining mould to texture the front and back of the leaf: place on the mould, fold the top over and apply gentle pressure. Wash and dry the mould, and dust with talcum powder.

Place the leaf on a cel pad and smooth the edges with a bone tool. Leave to dry. Dust with yellow and paprika powder food colouring, brushing from the edge to the centre of the leaf. Brush the front of the leaf with leaf-green powder, from the wire stem out to the edge of the leaf. Spray with fat or dip in glaze. Allow to dry.

For rain or dew drops, use black food colouring to paint one side of a droplet. Place clear piping gel in a paper piping bag and pipe a drop over the painted line. The black line will emphasize the rain drop. Piping gel will form a skin after drying for a few days.

Bind the wire of the leaves with green florists' tape. Bind the leaves together, placing the largest leaf at the top, followed by pairs of smaller leaves.

Use salmon-pink food colouring to colour a piece of flower paste to the deepest colour required. Cut the paste in half; wrap one piece in polythene and knead an equal amount of white paste into the second. Repeat to give three tints of paste.

Bend a hook at one end of 24-gauge wire. Thread the straight end of the wire through a ball of darkest colour paste until the hook is just buried. Shape the paste into a long slim cone; dry.

Select a cutter slightly larger than the cone. The same size cutter is used for the entire rose. Roll out the darkest paste as thinly as possible: you should be able to read through it. Cut out four petals. Cover with polythene. Place a petal on a cel pad and smooth a bone tool around the very edge so that the paste frills slightly. Cup the petal by gently rubbing the centre with the bone tool.

Paint softened flower paste on the petal. Lay the wired cone slightly off centre. The petal must be larger than the cone. Fold one side of the petal over the cone, tucking in the edge until the cone is concealed. Roll the other side tightly around the cone to form a bud. Frill and cup another petal. Brush softened paste on it, place the bud in the centre so that the top of the petals are the same height and wrap the petal tightly around the bud.

Brush lemon powder food colouring on the pointed ends of the third and fourth petals. Brush softened paste on their bottom halves and place the bud on the centre of the third petal. Secure the left side of the petal. Tuck the fourth petal into the third petal and wrap it around the bud. This will give the impression that the petals are entwined. This is a rose bud.

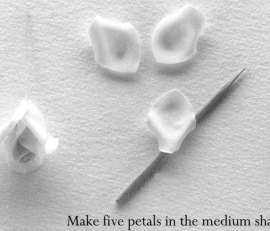

Make five petals in the medium shade. Cup and frill two petals. Dust with lemon powder food colouring, brush the bottom point with softened paste and secure to the rose as before. Frill and cup the remaining petals and dust with lemon. Curl

back the edges on a cocktail stick (toothpick). Brush just the points with softened paste and secure to the rose. The rose can be used or extra petals added: make six in the palest paste, colour with lemon and roll the petals. Brush softened paste on just the point of each, then dry slightly before securing to the rose. It is easier to attach the petals when holding the rose upside down.

Calyx: Roll out some moss-green flower paste and brush with white sparkle powder food colouring to give the silver effect found inside the calyx.

Select a cutter: each sepal on the calyx should be slightly smaller than the petal cutter. Cut out the calyx. Place on a cel pad and cup each sepal

with a bone tool. Using a scalpel, cut slivers of paste off the edge of each sepal for a feathery effect. Paint softened paste on the rose base. Thread the calyx onto the wire. Add a small ball of green paste to the back of the calyx for the rose hip. Carefully bend the calyx sepals back. Leave to dry.

Dust the edges of the petals with rose-pink powder food colouring – I recommend a wide chisel brush for this. Brush from the outside to the centre of the rose. Hold the rose over the steam of a boiling kettle.

SWEET PEA

SWEET PEA
Delicate summer flowers available in every shade and colour, including blue as well as red, pink, apricot, mauve, purple, cream, yellow and white.

Bend a large hook at the end of a piece of 26-gauge wire and push a small ball of white paste against the hook. Pinch the paste against the wire until the centre of the wire hook is filled with paste. Leave to dry.

   Roll out white flower paste as thinly as possible on a lightly greased board. Cut out a petal, see page 141. Place the petal on a cel pad and smooth the edges with a bone tool. Mark a line down the middle of the petal using the pointed end of a veining tool. Paint softened paste all over the petal. Position the wired centre on one half of the petal. Then fold the petal in half to enclose the wired centre. Tilt the tip back slightly. Leave to dry. Dust the petal with pink powder food colouring, brushing from the petal edge towards the wire.

FLOWER TIP
Although the flowers have a bright colour, I always begin by using pale paste, then dust the finished flowers to the depth of colour required. The result is more translucent than when using dark paste.

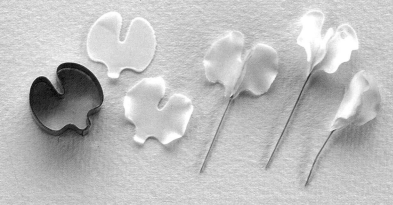

Use the second cutter, see page 141, to cut out a petal from thinly rolled white paste. Place the petal on a cel pad and frill the edge by rubbing it firmly with the wide end of a veining tool.

Paint a line of softened flower paste on the centre of the petal. Lay the dry wired petal down the middle. Pinch the back of the lower petal to ensure it is firmly secured. Leave to dry. Brush the frilled edges of the petal with pink powder food colouring.

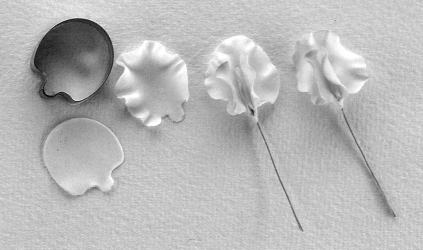

FLOWER TIP
Sweet peas are climbing plants and the flowers are not cut with foliage. Although there are no leaves, tendrils provide an interesting contrast in shape to the sugar flowers which have long, straight stems and are difficult to arrange.

Cut out the third petal, see page 141. Place it on a cel pad and frill the edges with the wide end of a veining tool. Paint a line of softened flower paste down the middle of the petal, then lay the wired flower on top. Press the back petal into position so that it is secured. Leave to dry. Brush pink powder food colouring on the frilled edge of the petal.

Calyx: Roll a ball of green flower paste, then pinch it between your thumb and finger to form a stem and a light bulb shape. Gently pinch the bulb of paste to flatten it, taking care to keep the stem in the middle. Place on a lightly greased board and roll out the paste as thinly as possible using a plastic dowel. Place the cutter, see page 141, over the stem and cut out the calyx.

Insert the point of a greased wooden dowel into the centre of the calyx. Push the dowel against your thumb and rotate the calyx until the centre forms a cone shape. Place the calyx on a cel pad and mark a line down the inside of each petal using the wide end of a veining tool. Paint inside the calyx with softened paste and thread it onto the flower, then secure to the sweet pea back.

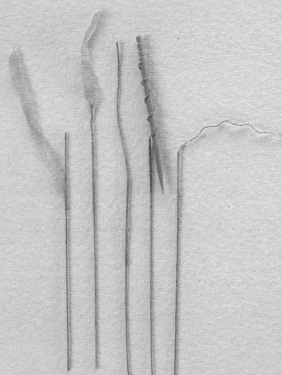

Tendril: Cut a piece of green paper florists' tape into 3mm × 12.5cm (⅛ × 5 inch) strips. Bind the strips to a piece of 26-gauge wire, 1cm (½ inch) from the top and continue to the top of the wire. Roll the tape between your finger and thumb twisting the pieces together. Wind the tape loosely around a cocktail stick (toothpick). Carefully slide the cocktail stick out to leave the tape curled.

Use half-width green paper florists' tape to bind the flowers together – they should be staggered in position down the stem. Use tweezers to bend the flower stems into natural curves.

Sweet peas are a delicate flower and the thin paste easily breaks. Colouring the petals as they are made reduces the risk of the brush catching and causing damage once the flower is assembled.

THE ARRANGEMENTS
Single-ended arrangement

11 fuchsia buds
24 fuchsia flowers
14 fuchsia leaves
30 eucalyptus leaves
14 lily-of-the-valley stems
4 bunches of ribbon loops

◄ Remove the paper from the back of a mini deco oasis and thread adhesive tape through the loops to form a cross. Stick the tape over a bouquet stand so that the oasis is firmly secured in place.

▶ Cut the first fuchsia stem to two-thirds of the length for the finished arrangement and the second stem to one-third of the finished length. Push the stems into the oasis. If the long stem is too heavy to be supported in the oasis, touch the end of the wire with a hot glue gun, then inset it into the oasis for extra stability.

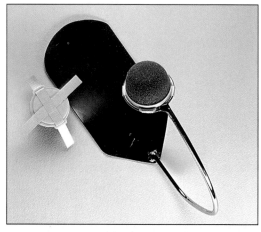

◀ Push ribbons and flowers into the oasis to form a tear-drop shape. The eucalyptus should form a single line from one side of the arrangement to the other.

FLOWER TIP
Mini deco oasis are available for fresh or dry arrangements. They are usually sold in packs of twelve. They have sticky backs for securing on a base or tape can be used to bind them if necessary.

87

▲ Always insert the stems pointing towards the centre: if a section could be cut through the wires, they should look like the spines of a fan. Push in the stems of the lily-of-the-valley between the eucalyptus leaves.

▲ Insert some short-stemmed flowers and leaves so that their backs touch the oasis. These will conceal the oasis and give depth to the arrangement.

▲ Wide ribbon loops have been used to bring light between the dark flowers. The loops help to define the flower shapes and prevent the arrangement looking heavy.

▲ Fill the centre of the arrangement with flowers and leaves. Look at the arrangement from all sides to check that there are no large holes or gaps.

BRIGHT FLOWERS MAKE A WONDERFUL DISPLAY ON THIS SIMPLE CAKE. DRAPING FUCHSIA FLOWERS CAN BE difficult to arrange – often when placed flat or wired into bouquets they look unnatural and out of place. By displaying them on a C-shaped stand from the rear, the fuchsias cascade naturally over the cake. Piped broiderie Anglais, a sugarpaste frill and fine ribbon complete the decoration.

Posy-pick spray

2 cymbidium orchids
14 ivy leaves
9 stephanotis buds
14 stephanotis flowers

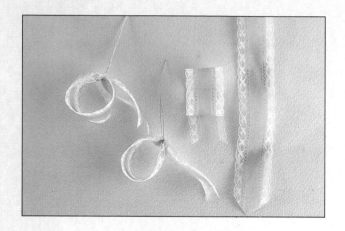

▲ Bind reel wire around looped lace and twist tightly. Cut the end of the lace in a 'V' shape. Make three loops. Insert a posy pick in the cake and fill with flower paste. Trim lace wires to 3.5cm (1½ inch); push into posy pick.

▲ Tape the flowers and leaves in bunches or natural-looking stems. Bend the stem of the ivy leaves at an angle and cut off the excess wire to 2.5cm (1 inch). Push the ivy into the posy pick.

◀ Push the stems of the stephanotis flowers into the paste, arranging them in a line across the top of the ribbon, with buds towards the ends.

◀ Push the stem of the orchid in the posy pick. Add extra stephanotis under the orchid petals to make a full spray of flowers. Place the second orchid behind the first.

The spray is shown on a cake on the title page.

Wired posy or bouquet

6 lily-of-the-valley flowers
5 azalea flowers
8 blue bell flowers
7 blue bell buds
11 chincherinchee flowers
10 rose leaves

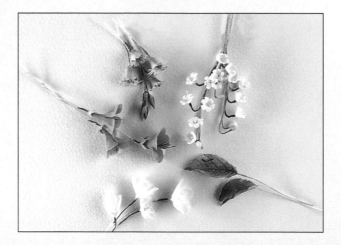

▲ Posy: Using 3mm (⅛ inch) wide ribbon, make three figure-of-eight loops the same length as the diameter of the posy. Make two stems of wired ribbon loops. Twist the three figure-of-eight loops together at the binding point to form a circle.

▲ Push the stem of a leaf through the ribbon, then bend the wire at a 90° angle so the tip of the leaf is in the same position as the ribbon. Arrange five leaves, five chincerinchee flowers and three blue bells to form the outside edge of the bouquet. Bind the wires together at the back of the posy.

◄ Keeping all the wires the same length, thread three lily-of-the-valley, three azalea and three chincherinchee flowers into the posy. Bind the flowers in place.

FLOWER TIP
If another return is added to the bouquet it can be made into a hogarth, or crescent, arrangement.

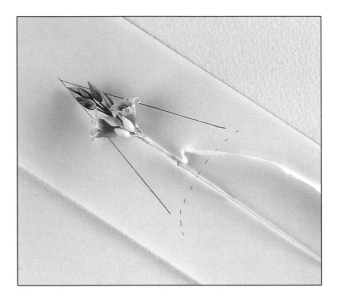

▲ Place three leaves in the centre of the bouquet against the binding wire to give the posy depth and cover the stems of the flowers. Tape three blue bells together and bind these in the centre of the posy to make the focal point. The posy must be domed in shape.

▲ Shower-Shaped Bouquet: The posy can be used at this stage or it may be developed into a shower-shaped bouquet. Draw a circle the diameter of the posy on a piece of paper. Mark the length required for the finished bouquet and draw lines from this mark to the sides of the circle. Begin by binding together five buds and two blue bell flowers to form the point of the triangle using full-width white parafilm tape.

▲ Bind the flowers to the central stem. Hold them against the drawing to check the length of the stems and the shape.

▶ When the triangular arrangement, or return, is complete, hold its stem against the posy. Bend the return stem at the point where the two stems cross, bind with reel wire and white parafilm tape.

TWO BOUQUETS OUTLINE THE HEART-SHAPED CAKES
and their points draw the attention towards
the inscription on the large cake. The two sloping
heart cakes are cut from one 20cm (8 inch) round
cake. The cake is sliced at an angle, then one layer
is turned upside down so that the sloping top of
each heart faces forward to provide the perfect
platform for the flower arrangements. The cakes
are trimmed with fine ribbon and strings of
pearls; tiny flower arrangements on the the corners
complete the decoration.

95

Semi-crescent bouquet

20 gold ivy leaves
28 holly leaves
18 holly berries
1 poinsettia

◀ Bend the stems of the ivy leaves to the required length of the bouquet. Use green parafilm tape to bind the ivy leaves to the poinsettia.

▲ Bind the holly leaves and berries onto stems, then bind them into the bouquet.

◀ Continue binding bunches of holly to the poinsettia, forming the crescent shape of the bouquet.

FLOWER TIP
A large bloom, such as lily or orchid, may be used instead of poinsettia in this arrangement.

▲ When binding the stems together, the aim is to keep the binding tape in one place and as close as possible to the back of the poinsettia – this is the binding point.

▲ Cut out some of the wire as close as possible to the binding point so that the stem is delicate enough to fit into a posy pick yet strong enough to hold the weight of the bouquet. Tape the wire stems together to make a handle.

▲ Cut a small hole in the cake coating: use the point of a small sharp knife, turning it in a circular movement to 'drill' the small hole; remove the sugarpaste and marzipan. Push a posy pick into the cake, leaving it high enough to be easily seen when the bouquet is removed.

▲ Place the handle of the bouquet into the posy holder. Remember to tell the recipient of the cake that the posy pick and wired flowers are not edible.

A LARGE FLOWER SURROUNDED BY FOLIAGE IS A SURE
recipe for success. This bold poinsettia is the focal
point for a stunning seasonal arrangement and
brush-embroidered cones complete the festive
centrepiece. The cake is positioned on a red runout
collar and the extension work emphasizes the shape.

Hogarth arrangement

14 ivy leaves
23 sweet peas

▲ Select a suitable container: I have used a silver trinket or jewellery box and placed layers of cardboard in the container to lift the dome of the mini deco oasis higher than the side of the box. The paper has been removed from the back of the oasis and it is firmly attached to the card.

▲ Cut the stems to the required length, then insert the sweet peas into the oasis, pointing the stems towards the centre of the oasis.

◀ Add single flowers and ivy leaves to the oasis, always pointing the wire towards the centre of the oasis. Keep the stems very short and cover the oasis, working from the edge to the centre.

◄ Use tweezers to hold the stems when the arrangement begins to fill. To reduce the number of breakages, care must be taken to put the short-stemmed flowers and leaves in the arrangement first, followed by the flowers with longer stems.

FLOWER TIP
A hogarth arrangement is a flat 'S' shaped design. Unlike a bouquet, an 'arrangement' does not have a stem to hold at the back; this is placed flat on a cake surface, not in a posy pick.

► Fill the centre of the arrangement with sweet peas. Look at the arrangement from all sides to check that there are no large holes and that the oasis is concealed.

THIS CAKE ILLUSTRATES AN ALTERNATIVE METHOD OF
displaying sugar flowers, by arranging them in a
silver trinket box which will become a lasting
keepsake of an important occasion.
The cake is double coated with sugarpaste
and templates are used to cut away the areas of
white sugarpaste to reveal the pink undercoating.
The effect is delicate and the result is a versatile
cake which is equally suitable for many occasions
– an anniversary, birthday, engagement
or adult christening.

Hogarth bouquet

4 primrose leaves
9 primrose flowers
5 bunches of mimosa, including 12 leaves
10 narcissus flowers
3 narcissus buds
6 freesia flowers • 11 freesia buds

▲ Bend the stems of the narcissi to the required length of the spray. Cut a long length of reel wire and wrap it tightly around the stems to form the binding point.

▶ Position two sprays of freesia to outline the narcissi and bind them in place to develop the shape of the bouquet. Bind the spray of mimosa in the centre: the height is important as the top of the mimosa should complete an imaginary curved line from one end of the bouquet to the next.

FLOWER TIP

A bouquet is an arrangement which is designed to be held. Sugar flower bouquets have a stem which is held in place on the cake in a posy pick.

▲ Bind the stems of the primroses to the bouquet. Place the primrose leaves on short wires behind the flowers to give depth to the bouquet and to attract attention away from the stems.

▲ If the stem is getting too thick, cut out some of the wire as close as possible to the binding point. Add extra flowers to fill the shape, positioning them to form lines or groups.

▲ Attach more flowers if required, making sure that the binding point does not move down the stem. Cut the end of the stem to about 5cm (2 inch).

▲ Make two wired ribbon bows and place them against the stem. Use full-width florists' tape to bind the stem into a neat handle.

▲ A posy pick must be used on the cake if the stem of the bouquet penetrates the coating.

SPRING FLOWERS SWEEP ACROSS THIS TWO-TIER
cake. The hogarth curve arrangement leads the
eye from the top of the fan-shaped cake, which is
positioned on an angled stand, down to the hearts
and flowers decorating the lower cake.
The delicate heart and flower design on the cake
side echoes the colours and choice of flowers used
in the arrangement – the perfect choice for a
spring wedding.

107

Unwired arrangement

7 brush-embroidered leaves (see below)

5 anemones

9 asters

▲ Place some softened paste in a piping bag, see page 6. Cut the wire as short as possible on the flowers. Pipe a small bulb of paste on the back of the flowers and secure them to the cake.

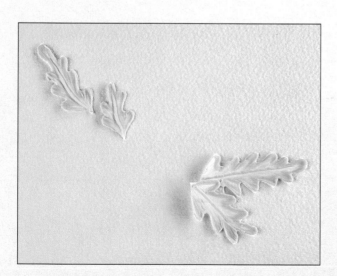

▲ The brush-embroidered leaves can be worked directly on the cake or they can be cut out of white flower paste and dried. Pipe green royal icing around the edge of the leaf and smooth it towards the middle with a wet brush. Leave to dry.

◄ Attach the asters to the cake before the anemones so that the arrangement will look full and interesting, and to avoid having large spaces under the flowers.

▲ The flowers look their best when they are grouped together. Place some flowers at an angle to add interest and to make the arrangement attractive from all angles.

▲ Use the asters to give depth and shape to the arrangement. Attach each flower to the cake with softened paste.

A FEW BOLD FLOWERS CREATE A STUNNING RESULT when bright colours are used. Had the flowers been worked in pastel tones, the design would not have been as eye-catching.

The pale green, royal icing collar makes the white icing on the cake appear very bright and clean, contributing to the bold impression made by the cake. Notice that the main flower arrangement is assembled on the collar rather than on the surface of the cake.

Corsage

24 freesia buds
6 freesia flowers
5 summer roses
7 rose leaves
10 jasmine buds
17 jasmine flowers

▲ Use half-width green parafilm tape to bind a stem of freesia and a stem of roses to a piece of 24-gauge wire to provide stability. The wire will be used as a base on which to bind all the other flowers.

▲ The flowers must be taped in natural groups — for example, freesia buds and flowers should be taped together to form a natural-looking stem of flowers. Tape rose leaves in groups of three or five. Do not tape different flowers together at this stage.

►Bind a stem of jasmine and rose leaves to the corsage, stretching the tape as much as possible. Place the leaves on short stems close to the binding wire to help conceal the taping and give depth to the corsage.

▲ Cut out excess wire from the stems if the corsage begins to look and feel heavy. Cut out only enough to prevent the stem being bulky – it must support the spray of flowers and not be flimsy.

▲ Continue to bind the flowers to the 24-gauge wire to form a triangle. The large rose forms the focal point of the bouquet and all stems after this point are bent back to form the other end.

▲ When the corsage has reached two-thirds of the required length, begin bending the stems of the flowers almost in half before taping them to the central wire.

▲ To finish the corsage, cut the stems to 2.5cm (1 inch) and tape them using full-width green parafilm tape. The stem of this type of bouquet does not have to be inserted in a posy pick, it is attached to the cake with soft flower paste and wires do not penetrate the coating. Place a bow over the end of the stem.

THE TALL BASKETTE OF FLOWERS PERFECTLY BALANCES
this four-tier cake design, providing height to lead
the eye towards the bell-shaped top tier and
attracting attention away from the cake stand.
The diamanté trims on the baskette hoop and in the
flower centres are matched by the trimming
between the heart-shaped extension work around
the sides of the cakes.

Baskette

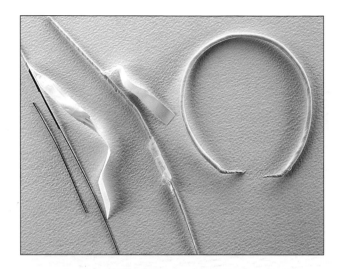

12 freesia buds
6 freesia flowers
8 summer roses
12 rose leaves
14 jasmine buds
14 jasmine flowers

▲ Use white parafilm tape to bind three lengths of 24-gauge wire together and pad with 2.5cm (1 inch) wide tissue paper. Bind with parafilm tape. Thread the wire into a stitched fabric tube which has one end sewn up. Stitch the open end. Bend the wire to form a curved handle.

Secure the second spray as for the first with a bulb of hot glue on the stem back. Place it on the arrangement to form a crescent. Cut the stems of the remaining flowers to length. Use a small bulb of the hot glue on the end of each wire to secure them to the centre of the arrangement.

▲ Cut out a disk of flower paste and dry. A string of diamanté can be twisted around the handle. Use a hot glue gun to secure the handle: it will only take a few seconds to dry in place. Using parafilm tape, bind rose buds to a stem of freesia. Continue taping flowers to form the spray for half the arrangement. Make an identical spray.

Note: Never use hot glue on a cake or any item to be eaten. It is safe to use it on items which will be removed from the cake.

Crescent arrangement

3 lilies
2 lily buds
6 Peruvian lily or alstroemeria buds
3 Peruvian lily or alstroemeria flowers
5 Peruvian lily or alstroemeria leaves
17 freesia buds
5 freesia flowers
2 bunches of ribbon loops

▲ Wire the Peruvian lily or alstroemeria buds, leaves and flowers together with half-width green paper florists' tape to form small sprays.

▲ Bind the freesia and a lily to the Peruvian lily or alstroemeria stem to form one end of the spray of flowers. Make a second identical spray.

◄ The back of the spray must be flat so that it will sit correctly on the cake.

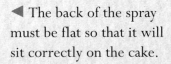

▲ Cut the stems of the sprays short and position them on the cake so that they just cross each other.

▲ Place a piece of flower paste over the crossed wires and arrange some loops of wired ribbon in the back of the bouquet.

▲ Assemble small flowers and buds under the lily petals, pushing the stems into the paste, to give the arrangement depth and prevent the paste from being seen.

▲ Place the third lily towards the back of the arrangement. The lilies should be arranged at different angles to create an attractive all-around display on the cake.

THREE LARGE LILIES IN DELICATE PINK AND LEMON
tones are combined with Peruvian lilies in the
graphic floral arrangement on this single-tier cake.
The dramatic impact of the flowers is enhanced by
the floating-effect created by positioning the cake
on a small cake board. The lace which trims the
bottom edge is dried in a curved position over a
rolling pin. It is carefully positioned a fraction
away from the surface of the board to avoid
damaging any of the pieces.

Crescent bouquet

7 dendrobium orchid buds
4 dendrobium orchid flowers
10 chrysanthemum buds
3 chrysanthemum flowers
3 chrysanthemum leaves
2 carnation buds
3 carnation flowers

▲ Tape the different varieties of flowers to pieces of 22-gauge wire. The aim is to keep the stems thin but they must be strong enough to hold the weight of the flowers.

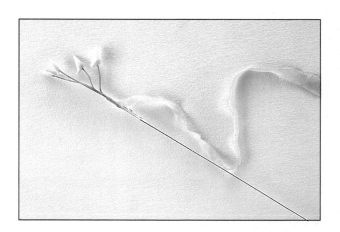

▲ Tape the buds of the dendrobium orchids together in two triangular shapes on two pieces of 22-gauge wire using half-width green paper florists' tape. The buds must be close enough together to hide the stem.

▲ Cut a length of reel wire and bind the stems of the dendrobium orchids together. Add chrysanthemums to the orchids.

The bouquet is held in the
figures' hand with hot glue.
Lay the figure down, pipe
the hot glue into the hand
and hold the bouquet in
place for 1–2 minutes.
A small piece of tape can be
bound over the hand and
stem for extra support.

▲ Bind the carnation stems to
the outside edge of the bouquet
to define the shape.

▲ Hold a stem of dendrobium orchids against the bouquet and bend the wire back to form the second side of the arrangement. Bind into place with reel wire.

▲ Continue binding the flowers to the bouquet. It is important to keep the binding wire in one place; if the wire travels down the stem, the bouquet will not have a good shape and it will be difficult to hide the stem.

▲ Cut the stem of the bouquet to about 5cm (2 inch) and bind it with green paper florists' tape.

Shower arrangements

30 agapanthus buds
20 agapanthus flowers
9 carnation leaves
6 carnation buds
10 carnation flowers
18 honeysuckle buds
33 honeysuckle flowers
6 honeysuckle leaves
9 pincushion or scabious flowers
3 pincushion or scabious buds
11 dendrobium orchid flowers
20 dendrobium orchid buds

◄ Make six bunches of wired lace loops and nine bunches of white pearls.

► Bind small bunches of flowers and buds together to form natural-looking stems of flowers. Use only one variety of flower on each stem; for example agapanthus buds and flowers, not carnation buds and agapanthus flowers.

◀ Hold the flower stems in your left hand and position them to form a triangular-shaped spray of flowers: this is called a *return*. When the flowers are in position bind the stems together with green paper florists' tape.

▲ Hold the return to the cake and bend the stem wire so the flowers cascade over the edge of the cake. Cut the stem to the required length, place it on the cake and push a ball of well-kneaded flower paste over it to hold the flowers firmly on the cake top.

▲ Add the loops of lace and pearls to give the arrangement depth and to contrast with the flowers. Push the stems of the flowers into the flower paste to create the size and shape of the arrangement.

▲ Fill the centre of the arrangement with flowers. Use tweezers to push the stems into the paste as this will help to avoid breakages to those flowers already in place.

CASCADING BOUQUETS ARE ARRANGED TO CREATE A balanced result on this beautiful three-tier wedding cake. Had the bouquets been positioned on the same side of each cake, the opposite side of the assembled cakes would have been quite bare. The strong shapes and colours of the flowers used in the bouquets are complemented by the bold embroidery design worked on the sides of the cakes. Fine embroidery would not have made as much impact and the cake would have looked unbalanced.

Symmetric arrangement

7 *chincherinchee centres*

14 *chincherinchee flowers*

7 *forget-me-not flowers*

4 *aster leaves*

5 *chrysanthemum leaves*

7 *single chrysanthemum flowers*

▲ Bind some 24-gauge wire with ribbon, then use a hot glue gun to glue strips of pearls to the wire. Cut a 10cm (4 inch) length of wire and bend it to form a loop.

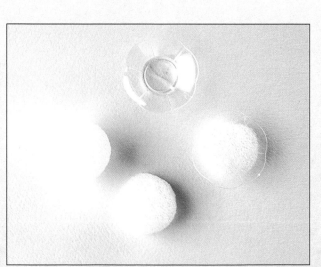

▲ Cut a polystyrene ball in half. Use a hot glue gun or double-sided adhesive tape to secure one half polystyrene ball to a favour or bonbonière cup.

▲ Cut three chrysanthemum leaves to the height of the arrangement for the left and right sides. Hold the ends of the wire on the glue gun, then push them into the polystyrene ball to form a triangle. The glue will hold the stems securely and prevent the arrangement coming apart.

▲ Place three loops of ribbon and pearls into the polystyrene. Outline the shape of the triangle with chincherinchee centres.

▲ Use tweezers to help push the wire stems into the polystyrene. Point all the stems to the centre of the arrangement.

▲ Cut some flower wires very short and insert them to cover the polystyrene. Turn the arrangement around and add flowers to cover the polystyrene but do not overdecorate the back of the arrangement with large flowers as this may prevent it from sitting against the side of the cake.

▲ Complete the arrangement by pushing small flowers into any spaces.

RIBBON AND PEARL HOOPS BRING MOVEMENT TO THE NEAT FLOWER ARRANGEMENTS ON THIS TWO-TIER cake. The kidney-shaped tiers are both cut from the one large oval cake: by cutting a comma-shaped piece of cake, the larger portion which remains forms the bottom tier. The small comma piece is turned upside down to form the top tier. The simple decoration consists of a pink frill covered by a white frill in which heart-shapes have been cut using a heart-shaped lace cutter. The overall effect is delicate yet quite definite.

Basket

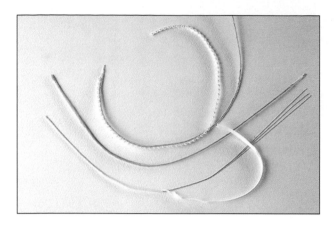

▲ Tape three pieces of 24-gauge wire together and bind with 5mm (¼ inch) wide ribbon. Use a hot glue gun to stick strips of pearls to one side of the wire. Bend the wire around a suitable-size bottle into a curve. Use a hot glue gun to stick the handle ends to a favour or bonbonière cup.

▲ Mix equal amounts of flower paste and sugarpaste. Roll out as thinly as possible and cut out two scalloped circles; a garrett frill cutter is ideal for this. Frill the edges of the paste with a cocktail stick (toothpick). Brush softened paste in the centre of one circle and stick the other on top. Brush softened paste on the back of the bonbonière cup and place on the frills to make a basket; dry.

3 chincherinchee centres
9 chincherinchee flowers
8 forget-me-not flowers
3 aster leaves
3 chrysanthemum leaves
4 single chrysanthemum flowers

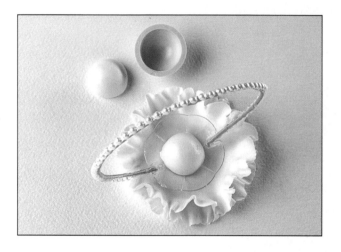

▲ Fill a ball mould with the remaining paste. Remove paste from the mould and stick it to the cup with softened paste.

▲ Cut the stems of three chincherinchee flowers so that the heads of the flowers do not extend beyond the frilled edge of the base.

▲ Form the posy shape with 3 chrysanthemum leaves and 3 chincherinchee centres with all the stems pointing to the centre. Place one flower in the centre.

▲ Add extra flowers. The loops of pearls are made by binding the two ends of lengths of the pearl strips with reel wire. Trim the wire to 1cm (½ inch). Push the wire into the paste.

► Continue adding forget-me-nots and small flowers to form a dome-shaped posy.

GLOSSARY

Airbrush A piece of artists' equipment, used for applying a thin, even coating of liquid colour. The colour may be faded from one area to another or around the edge in a vignette effect when using an airbrush. Available from art shops and sugarcraft suppliers.

Arrangement An arrangement of flowers is intended to lie flat on a cake surface unlike a bouquet which has a stem and is supported in a posy pick.

Ball Tool A sugarcraft modelling tool with a rounded end. Useful for cupping petals and hollowing areas of paste.

Baskette A delicate and decorative, basket-style container.

Bind To cover wire with floristry tape. The tape should be stretched as much as possible so that it sticks to itself. Stretching tape also gives finer results.

Binding Point The centre of a bouquet. This is the point where the wire used to secure the flowers is bound together to form a bouquet.

Bonbonière or Favour Cup A small receptable for holding the traditional confectionary gift presented to ladies at a wedding.

Bone Tool A sugarcraft modelling tool with ball-shaped ends in two sizes. Useful for cupping small petals and thinning areas of paste.

Bouquet An arrangement of flowers with a stem which is held in the hand or, in the case of sugar flowers, supported in a posy pick.

Calyx The calyx is the outer part of the flower found below the petals. It is usually green and made up of small leaf-like parts which are known as sepals.

Chisel Brush A paintbrush with bristles cut in a flat, squared end.

Corsage A small flower arrangement originally designed and shaped to fit on the bodice of a dress.

Column In an orchid, the column is the part of the flower which is made up of the stamens.

Dowel Pencil-like strips of different thicknesses and lengths. Wooden dowel from timber merchants can be cut into short lengths and sharpened with a pencil sharpener. Plastic dowel sold for sugarcraft work is used for rolling out small or delicate areas of paste.

Florists' Tape Available in many colours and different types. Used by florists, this is also an important item of equipment when making and arranging sugar flowers, see page 10.

Hogarth Hogarth is a term used to describe arrangements or bouquets in the form of a double curve or 'S' shape.

Hot Glue Gun Available from craft suppliers or do-it-yourself stores, this is an appliance for applying quick-setting hot glue. The glue is NOT EDIBLE and it must not be used directly on any surface which is in contact with the cake.

Labellum This is the larger, lower petal of an orchid which gives the flower its distinctive appearance.

Leaf Node The small swelling from which leaves grow on the plant stem.

Mini Deco Oassis A small semi-sphere of oasis attached to a plastic base.

Modelling Clay Craft clay or dentists' modelling clay which may be used to take an impression of parts of a flower. The manufacturer's instructions should be followed for setting the impression, usually by baking, then the piece of clay may be used as a mould for flower paste.

Parafilm Tape A type of florists' tape, used for binding flower stems.

Petal Usually the most conspicuous part of a flower, intended to attract the attention of pollinating insects. Petals vary enormously in number, size, shape and colour according to the flower.

Pollen The tiny grains or powder on the stamens of a plant. For sugar flowers, manufactured pollen can be purchased in a variety of colours, including speckle pollen which is speckled rather than uniform in colour. Pollen may also be made, see page 9.

Posy A rounded arrangement.

Posy Pick A small container for holding the stem of a flower arrangement. A posy pick is inserted through the coating and into a cake. It prevents the wires from coming in contact with the edible part of the cake.

Return This term is used in floristry to describe a triangular-shaped area of flowers which forms part of a bouquet or larger arrangement.

Scalpel Also known as a craft knife. A cutting instrument with a very sharp, fine, disposable blade. Essential for precise work.

Seedhead A head of seeds formed on the top of the plant.

Seedpod A pod or area in which the seed develops. Seedpods are often found below the flower.

Sepal This is one small part of the calyx.

Shower Arrangement or Bouquet A shower arrangement or bouquet consists of a full, rounded area of flowers leading to a point, or a return.

Softened Flower Paste A mixture used as a glue in sugar work, see page 6.

Stamen The pollen-bearing parts of the flower.

Stigma The part of the flower which receives the pollen from the stamens. The stigma is at the top of the pistil.

Tendril The slim, trailing part of a climing plant which anchors the plant as it grows up an object.

Throat The term is used for the deepest area of a flower, especially when the petals form a trumpet shape.

Veiners Sugarcraft tools designed for making leaf impressions in paste. There are many types available with specific patterns for different types of leaves. Some are single veiners which make a one-sided impression in the paste and there are also double-sized veiners which are closed onto a piece of paste to make realistic impressions on both sides of the paste leaf.

Veining Tool A sugarcraft modelling tool for marking veins and other lines on paste.

Templates for cutters

The templates on the following pages are outlines of cutters used to stamp out various parts of the flowers. If using the templates, trace them carefully and use a scalpel to cut out the shape as cleanly as possible. Alternatively, cutters may be purchased from sugarcraft suppliers.

BLUE BELL, see page 22

Flowers

Inner petal

Outer petal

Leaf

LILY,

Peruvian or alstroemeria, see page 55

ANEMONE, see page 16

Flower

Leaves and
Calyx

Calyx

Flower

ASTER, see page 18

Leaf

Calyx

Petal

Leaf

CARNATION, see page 24

Flowers

CHINCHERINCHEE, see page 27

Leaf

Calyx

CHRYSANTHEMUM, single, see page 32

AZALEA, see page 20

N6

N4

N2

Leaf

EUCALYPTUS, see page 34

N5

N3

N1

Leaf

CHRYSANTHEMUM, double, see page 30

FORGET-ME-NOT, see page 36

FREESIA, see page 38

Flower

Leaves

Leaves

HOLLY, see page 44

FUCHSIA, see page 41

Leaves

Leaf

IVY, see page 48

JASMINE, see page 50

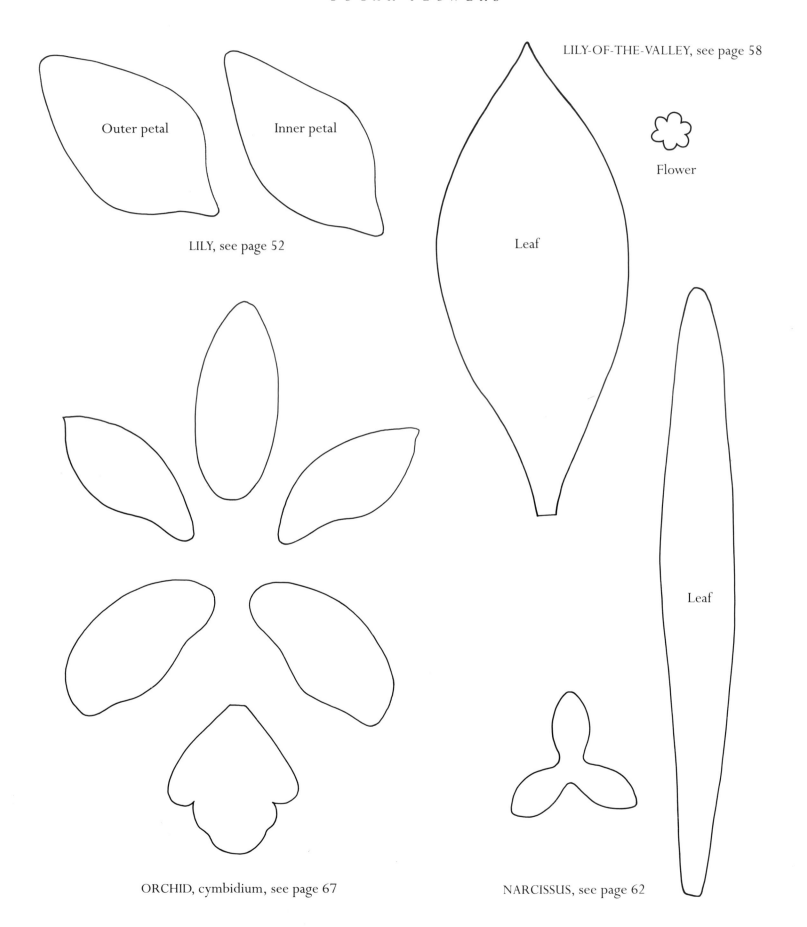

Outer petal

Inner petal

LILY, see page 52

LILY-OF-THE-VALLEY, see page 58

Flower

Leaf

Leaf

ORCHID, cymbidium, see page 67

NARCISSUS, see page 62

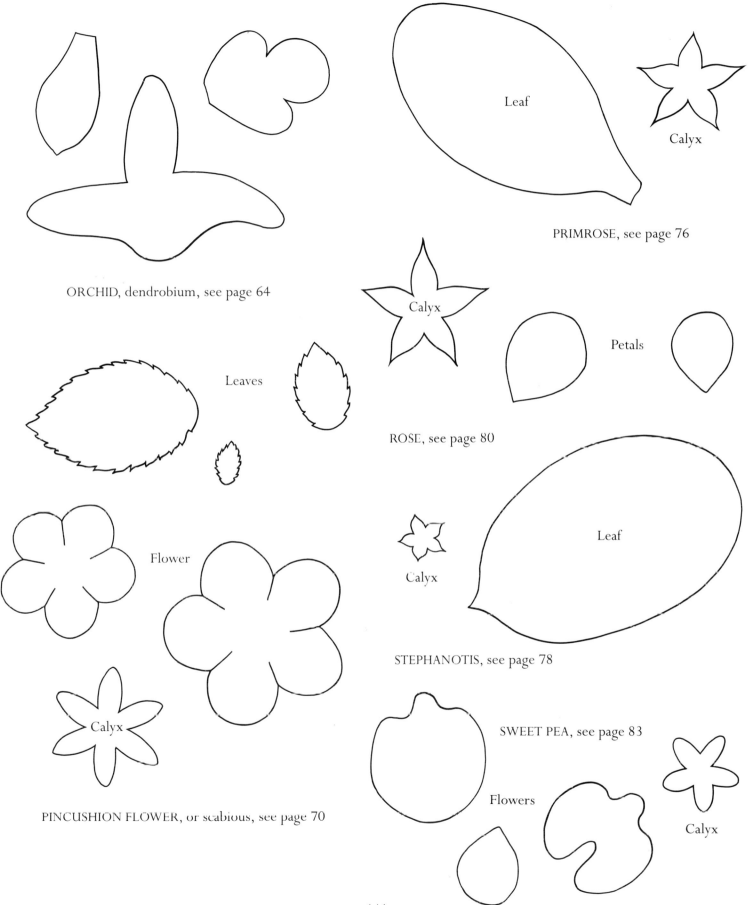

ORCHID, dendrobium, see page 64

PRIMROSE, see page 76

Leaf

Calyx

Calyx

Leaves

ROSE, see page 80

Petals

Flower

Leaf

Calyx

STEPHANOTIS, see page 78

Calyx

SWEET PEA, see page 83

PINCUSHION FLOWER, or scabious, see page 70

Flowers

Calyx

Index

ACKNOWLEDGEMENTS

Special thanks to Sue Ballard for your
invaluable support.

*The author and publishers would like to thank the following
for their assistance:*

A. O. K. Metals, 16 Queensland Road,
Bournemouth, BH5 2AB.

Cake Art Ltd, Venture Way, Crown Estate, Priorswood,
Taunton, Somerset, TA2 8DE.

Cel Cakes, Springfield House, Gate Helmsley,
York, YO4 1NF.

Guy, Paul & Co. Ltd, Unit B4, Foundry Way,
Little End Road, Eaton Socon, Cambs. PE19 3JH.

Hamilworth Floral Products Ltd., 23 Lime Road,
Dumbarton, Dumbartonshire, Scotland, G82 2RP.

J.F. Renshaw Ltd., Crown Street, Liverpool, L8 7RF
for supplying Regalice.

Occasions Florist, 169 South Street, Romford,
Essex, RM1 1PS.

Orchard Products, 51 Hallyburton Road, Hove,
East Sussex, BN3 7GP.

PME Sugarcraft, Brember Road, South Harrow, HA2 8UN.

Rainbow Ribbons, Unit D5, Seed Bed Centre, Davidson
Way, Romford, Essex, RM7 0AZ.

Squires Kitchen, Squires House, 3 Waverley Lane,
Farnham, Surrey, GU9 8BB.

Tinkertech Two, 40 Langdon Road, Parkstone, Poole,
Dorset, BH14 9EH.

Twins Wedding Shop, Victoria Road, Romford, Essex.